The *Joy* of *Missions*

50 Years of Ministry Seen from the Lighter Side

The *Joy* of *Missions*

50 Years of Ministry Seen from the Lighter Side

Flay Allen

Piedmont, South Carolina

CTS Publications, LLC

The Joy of Missions
Copyright © 2016 by Flay Allen

All Scripture quotations, unless otherwise indicated, are taken from the Authorized King James Version.

Editorial team: Renee Russell, Dennis Flower, Andy Bonikowsky, David Bonikowsky
Design and page layout: Andy Bonikowsky, David Bonikowsky

Printed in the United States of America

ISBN: 978-0-9886056-2-6

Dedication

I dedicate this book to my lifelong friend and traveling buddy, Frank Giles Buie, who has a heart for missions. His vision and encouragement has inspired many missionaries as they have taken the joyous message of the Gospel to the needy multitudes. He also founded Faith Christian Missions, which has been assisting missionaries around the world for over 40 years. His investment in our ministry has exceeded anything within our dreams. Thanks, Frank.

Table of Contents

Additional Blessings

A View From Our Daughters

Foreward

Everybody loves an encourager because everybody loves to be encouraged. And thankfully, most of us can think of someone we would describe as this sort of person. He or she is that relative or friend you are always glad to see, the one who brightens your day, who continually directs your attention to the good side of things instead of the bad.

My father-in-law is this kind of man.

As a missionary kid in Spain, I came to know "Uncle Flay"— now, Dad Allen—not just as the father of three sisters who lived some hours away, but as one of the happiest men I knew.

His greeting was always with a smile and a touch of good humor. He seemed to thrill in building others up and inspiring them to serve the Lord with their talents. He was a natural "life of the party", and yet, not in the unpleasant way of a selfish man, hungry for attention.

His optimistic attitude was the out working of his faith, expressing itself in the day to day of life. He simply believed that being God's child was a positive and happy privilege. He lived as though Romans 8:28 were etched onto his eyes so that it's truth could be immediately applied to every situation. Everything was good because God had brought it to him.

That daily perspective turned each obstacle into a creative challenge and an opportunity to look to God for help and wisdom. Instead of responding to a disappointment by groaning and complaining he was instantly thinking of solutions, and even ways to improve the original situation if possible.

Good humor was seldom far from the surface, though he kept it wisely guarded with strong convictions. Most of those who know him well have learned to wait just a tiny little bit, whenever he starts to tell a story or make an observation. And why this caution? Because if not, you will sooner or later catch yourself looking at him in dead seriousness, only to have him suddenly flip the perspective to show that he was totally joking!

I am quite certain that many friends will be nodding their heads with approval as they read these words. Whether their experience with him was in Spanish or English, in the Americas or Europe, in the ministry or not, they will heartily agree with the following statement:

Flay Allen's consistent testimony of living happily with the Lord Jesus has earned him full credibility to share this collection of personal anecdotes. His joy in Christ is the bright thread that joins them all into a single story, one that he hopes will give all glory to Whom it belongs, the Master of missions.

Andy Bonikowsky — July 2016

Introduction

Since retiring from active foreign mission work in October of 2013, several people have asked if I am going to write a book. Frankly, I had never given the idea much thought. As you know, there are dozens of great missionary biographies already out there, and most of them are very challenging and serious. I have been blessed by reading many of them. Far greater challenges, blessings, and victories than those Margaret and I have experienced can be found in any number of existing biographies.

I do admit that I have not been a prolific correspondent and that I have been lax in communicating victories and blessings to my family. Our children (Debbie, Becky and Mimi) will remember many of the highlights of our early ministry both in Chile and Spain. My son-in-law, Andy Bonikowsky, and Mimi returned to Spain as missionaries shortly after marriage and have been able to follow our later ministry quite closely in Spain.

Unfortunately, my other son-in-law, Drew Martin, who is pastor of a Baptist church in South Carolina, has only been able to visit us once in Spain. Drew has made it possible for his wife Becky, a nurse, to visit Mimi, her twin sister, occasionally. Drew and Becky's daughters, Jennifer and

Caroline, have seen very little of the ministry in Spain. I regret that I have not shared more details with them.

Our single daughter, Debbie, returned to Spain for six months to teach a one-semester public speaking course in our Bible Institute and also to help me publish a book of hymn arrangements for classical guitar. But she, too, missed out on a lot which occurred during our final years in Spain.

Even where I have shared the blessings and victories in our ministry, I have usually omitted the failures. Additionally, there have been many humorous events which I have chosen not to publish in prayer letters. I have heard it said, however, that if a missionary does not have a sense of humor, he won't last long on the mission field. I thank the Lord for giving me a sense of humor, although I recognize that some in our family, and especially Margaret, often get embarrassed by it.

Just recently I commented to some friends that Margaret doesn't always appreciate my sense of humor. Without missing a beat, Margaret said, "It's just that I have got sense, and Flay has got humor!" Be that as it may, on many occasions, we have had to laugh at ourselves.

By God's grace, Margaret and I have enjoyed 52 years on the field. The Lord has given us tremendous blessings, although we have seen our share of failures. We have rejoiced, and we have wept. But we have also laughed a lot. For what has been accomplished, we give God all the credit.

Recently, I have had some very interesting conversations with Bronner, my oldest brother. He told me that since he had returned to Greenville from Cheyenne, Wyoming, where he lived for nearly 10 years after retiring, he had gotten to know Alton (my youngest brother). He continued "Now that you have retired, I would like to get to know you." Then he added that he would like to know more about the work that we have done on the mission field.

I suppose the best way to tell the story is to write a book. So, for my family and a few close friends (or should I say for our extended family), here goes. It will be primarily a collection of "missionary stories" narrated from memory as best I can recall them. Some have been exciting and encouraging; others have been frustrating and discouraging. Some, in my opinion, have been downright funny. For any who might think that a missionary has to always be serious, let me warn you up front that quite a few of the stories I describe should probably fall into the category of what I call "the lighter side of missions."

Please feel free to rejoice, weep, or laugh.

Flay Allen

US, CUBA, AND MEXICO

ONE
Outsmarted by my Pastor

IT WAS a lovely summer Sunday afternoon. I was a happy and contented high school graduate. My parents had invited the pastor and his wife, Gene and Lucille Fisher, for lunch. Our dinner conversation had produced all kinds of pleasantries, so I was totally unsuspecting and unarmed for what was about to come. Then it happened.

My pastor took me into another room for a private conversation beginning with, "Flay, I think you should go to Bob Jones University this fall."

Such a plan had not been in my thinking, and I was somewhat shocked by the suggestion. I immediately responded, "I can't go."

Typical of my pastor, who was also a professor, he simply said, "Give me three reasons why you can't go."

My first reason was very clear. "I don't have the money."

"I have a job for you. You can start work in the morning and earn enough money to get you started. Now let's hear your second reason."

Trying to muster up a bit of boldness, I said, "Pastor, I don't think I could put up with all the high-folutin' music down there."

I thought Pastor Fisher should have realized that I was pure country and bluegrass. My brothers and I formed part of a musical group, and my mother was very proud of the fact that her "boys were playing over the radio." In fact, we had been invited to go to Nashville and play on the "Grand Ole Opry." Roy Acuff and his sidekick, Oswald, had given us the invitation, but they would never think of looking for me down at Bob Jones University!

But Pastor just asked me, "Do you really think it would hurt you to put the guitar down for a year and listen to their music?"

He just didn't leave much room for argument. I answered, "Well no, it probably wouldn't hurt me."

"Okay, now let's hear your third reason."

I was getting a bit uncomfortable, but answered, "Pastor, I just don't think I'm smart enough to go to college."

After putting his head down to think for what seemed like half a minute or 45 seconds, he responded, "Well, you just about got me on that one! But couldn't you just go and give it a try? And do your best?"

"Well, I guess so."

Then he said, "That's all God expects of you. Pack a suitcase; we're going to Greenville this afternoon."

"But Pastor, I'll have to talk to my Dad first."

"No, I've already talked to your Dad. Pack a suitcase. We're going to Greenville."

So, I packed a suitcase.

We jumped into his '49 Plymouth, and he actually let me drive to Greenville. (Now that made me feel like a university graduate!) When we hit the four-lane highway, we pulled the overdrive lever and cruised right down to Bob Jones University for my freshman year of college.

Thank you, Pastor Fisher.

Two
Don't Forget Philippians 4:19

M Y EXCITEMENT soared when a young Mexican evangelist, Evelio Perez, invited me to go to Cuba during the summer of 1957 and play the accordion for a mission team he was forming. I was in my junior year at Bob Jones University (BJU), and as usual, had no money. But I told him to give me a week to pray about it, and I would give him an answer. Apart from the money problem, I didn't have an accordion—and I didn't know how to play the accordion!

Nevertheless, I called my older sister, Violet, who was teaching school in Pensacola, Florida. I asked if she would buy me an accordion and let me pay for it after my graduation. Well, she responded like good sisters are supposed to respond and said "YES."

Our newly-formed team of three spent the next three months doing deputation on the weekends to raise funds for the summer.

Batista was president of Cuba at that time, and the country was going through a difficult time of financial crisis and political unrest. Fidel Castro was in the mountains consolidating his revolutionary army. But when we arrived in Cuba, in an ambience of turmoil and uncertainty, we found that hearts were open to the message of the Gospel. Missionary Roy Ackerle scheduled our meetings throughout the island. We had tent meetings, church campaigns, and were even invited to preach to the workers in a cigar factory! The Lord blessed, and we saw more than 300 professions of faith that summer.

Unfortunately, Evelio calculated our projected expenses based on the Mexican economy where the cost of living was less than half what it was in Cuba in 1957. Before summer was over, we were almost out of money and still needed to get home. We purchased Evelio's ticket to Mexico. Thomas Fowler and I had return tickets to get us and the station wagon we had taken for transportation to Key West, Florida, but we didn't have enough money for gas (let alone food) to get back to Pensacola.

As we were standing at the dock waiting to board the ferry, Brother Ackerle pulled the New Testament out of my shirt pocket, casually looked at it, then put it back. When we prayed and said goodbye, Brother Ackerly said, "Don't forget Philippians 4:19." We thanked him and boarded the ferry.

As we pulled out of the dock, he again yelled, "Don't forget Philippians 4:19."

About 20 minutes later, I asked Thomas if he knew what Philippians 4:19 said. He didn't, and neither did I. So when I took out the New Testament and opened it to Philippians chapter 4, there was a neatly folded $10 bill! I memorized Philippians 4:19 then and there, and I have never forgotten it!

We were excited and joyful. But even with gas just under 30 cents per gallon, we knew that we still didn't have enough money for the 800-mile drive to Pensacola.

We had stayed with a lovely couple in Fort Pierce, Florida, on the way down, so we headed there and arrived in town at 4:30 a.m. We waited until about 6:30 a.m. and then called them to give a report on the summer campaign. The lady asked if we had eaten breakfast, and since we had not, she invited us over for bacon and eggs!

As we told the couple of God's blessings (without mentioning the financial situation) the lady got tears in her eyes. She said "We have prayed for you, but we should have helped you financially. If we write a check now, will you accept it?" They wrote us a check for $15.00. We thanked them, hugged them, said goodbye, and drove straight to the bank. When the bank opened, we cashed our big check.

Rejoicing in God's provision and wonderful blessings during the summer, we headed to Pensacola. God had provided money for gas plus a few hamburgers along the way!

THREE

My Three Best Decisions

JUST WHERE does the road to missions begin? Mine started when I was 16, in a little country church near Chesnee, South Carolina. Perhaps it should have started eight years earlier when my mother and I stood beside the bed of my grandfather, Rev. Samuel P. Jones. For many years he was a circuit riding preacher and also principal of the country school. Grandpa Jones called me to his bedside and asked me, "How old are you, Samuel?" (He was the only one in our entire family that called me Samuel. I was "Flay" to everybody else.)

I answered, "I am eight years old."

Then Grandpa said, "Samuel, you are just about half old enough to enter seminary and begin studying to be a preacher."

I was very timid, and I don't think I answered Grandpa. A few weeks later, he went on to be with his Lord.

However, eight years later, the same church that my Grand-dad had started near Chesnee called Gene Fisher as pastor. Very soon, Pastor Fisher scheduled a guest speaker for revival meetings. By the week's end, I was under deep conviction, and at the end of the service, I made a decision. I knew I was a sinner and that Christ died for my sin. So I prayed a simple prayer and asked God to forgive me and save me. And He did. I didn't realize at the time that it was the most important decision I would ever make.

Fast forward about six years to an exciting and fruitful mission trip to Cuba. I saw firsthand a great need for the Gospel. I saw lives being transformed as dozens of people came forward to accept Christ. God gave me a love for Cuban people, and even though I was struggling with Spanish, I was able to communicate with hungry people and share the love of God with them. A year later on a mission trip to Mexico, I said "yes" to the missionary call—my second best decision.

During my freshman year at BJU, I met a charming Miss Margaret Amerson from Dothan, Alabama. She was sweet and beautiful. I thought, "She could easily be Miss Alabama." In the spring of 1959, my third best decision was to ask her to marry me. She said, "yes"! We were married in September, 1959, and started our first term of missionary service together in February, 1960. Through 52 years on the mission field, my Miss Alabama has stood by my side, supporting and encouraging me.

I just praise God for guiding me through my three most important decisions!

FOUR
South of the Border

TRAVELING IN Cuba with the evangelistic team in 1957 was a life-changing experience for me. I began praying about what the Lord would have me do the following summer. I also determined that, with the Lord's help, I would "dig into Spanish" and learn the colorful, poetic language of Cervantes.

As I began my senior year of studies at BJU, my college buddy from Guatemala, René Zapata, and I started praying and organizing a "Christ's Harvesters" evangelistic team to have meetings in Mexico during the summer of 1958. From our team of six members, we formed a brass trio and a vocal quartet. René planned to do most of the preaching, and I would play the accordion. At the last minute, my youngest brother, Alton Allen, who was still in high school, joined us with his trombone to take the place of one team member who had to cancel due to sickness in the family.

René was able to go on to Mexico early and schedule ten weeks of meetings, while our team traveled on the weekends to churches throughout the Carolinas and Georgia raising support for the summer trip. After the euphoria of college graduation was over (I graduated *magna cum lucky*), we packed our suitcases and instruments for our trip to the Rio Grande. Our first stopover was Pensacola, Florida, where we were joined by my brother, Alton.

René set our rendezvous at the "Abraham Lincoln" monument in Monterrey for Wednesday at 3:00 p.m. (Actually, the statue was of José González, a famous doctor in Mexico, but seated in a big chair, he looked a lot like Abraham Lincoln.) René left the state of Veracruz (a thousand miles south of Monterrey) on Monday morning, and we left Pensacola, Florida (about a thousand miles northeast of Monterrey) on Monday morning. René arrived at the monument at 3:05 p.m., and we arrived at 3:10 p.m.! We concluded that we were off to a good start!

We then shifted into high gear and headed to the pastor's house with 30 minutes to change clothes and get to a new mission church, in perhaps the poorest section of Monterrey, for our first service. We were served dinner first and then had a preaching service.

Let me make it clear that during our ten weeks of meetings all the way across Mexico, for the most part the food was delicious, but spicy—as in "hot!" Even in the poorest of homes, the people were accommodating, and the food was clean and tasty.

Our very first meeting, however, was an exception to the rule. The house was dirty. We ate in a patio along with the pigs and chickens, and we were inundated by a huge swarm of flies. I distinctly remember dipping a fly out of my beverage and also out of my soup. Fortunately, René had taught us that the missionary's prayer is "Where He leads me I will follow; What He feeds me I will swallow." No one in the team complained.

The Lord was looking out for us. The pastor's son was a medical doctor and quite familiar with the common ailments of foreign travelers. Sure enough, half of our team experienced the most frequent malady within the first 48 hours. The American tourists call it "Montezuma's Revenge." I have also heard it called "The Aztec Two-step!"

We saw a good harvest of souls in almost every church where we had meetings. Our only food problems came from our first meeting, and the only disturbances came during our third meeting, in San Luis, Potosí. We were warned that the priest had told people not to attend our services and that we should be prepared for trouble. Some of the men from the church stayed outside to control things. A few rocks were thrown at the building, but the service was not interrupted.

From there, we had services in Mexico City. We took time to visit the famous Basilica of Guadalupe. We were saddened to see dozens of people crawling toward the church, with their knees bleeding in some cases, as they pressed forward, hoping to at least reach the statue of the Virgin and kiss her toe.

After leaving Mexico City, we crossed the more than 10,000-foot high pass (Río Frío) on our way to Puebla. As we drove by and saw for the first time God's handiwork displayed in the beautiful twin volcanos, Popocatepetl and Iztaccihuatl, both above 17,000 feet tall, I was once again reminded that *the heavens declare the glory of God, and the firmament showeth His handiwork.* Then a couple of weeks later we were fascinated when we saw Mexico's highest volcanic mountain, the impressive Mt. Orizaba, with its 18,000-foot perfectly conical snow-capped peak.

Our meetings took us all the way down to the state of Tabasco. We were able to reach some of the towns by car and others on horseback or walking. But in each of the meetings, God blessed in the salvation of souls.

In Puebla we had some serious discussions with both René Zapata and Evelio Perez. God had burdened their hearts for evangelism in Mexico. The doors were wide open. They were receiving more invitations for meetings than they could possibly fulfill. They told me they needed an accordion player to accompany them in their meetings. I was excited about the possibility of becoming a full-time missionary. I told them that I would pray about it; however, I needed to get a job and pay off some college debts.

Besides, there was that indescribable feeling in my heart and mind, that it is not good that a man should be alone. My mind and heart seemed to be drawn to a beautiful Miss Margaret Amerson, who I met at BJU during my freshman year.

I should mention that before our trip began, one of the men who traveled with us that summer was convinced that God had called him to be a missionary. By the time the trip was over, he admitted that missions was not for him. I can't help but think that, had he not taken the missions trip with us, he would have probably been a one-term missionary.

Our ten weeks were over all too soon, but we rejoiced in the fact that the fruits of our efforts would be eternal. Hundreds of needy souls were born into the family of God that summer.

Church after church invited us to come back for future meetings. We promised them that we would pray about it.

I not only prayed about it; I prayed about returning to Mexico full-time.

FIVE
101 Dollars

AFTER MARGARET and I were married in September, 1959, we immediately started deputation to raise our support to join the evangelistic team in Puebla, Mexico. Our monthly support figure had been set at $200.00.

In January, 1960, with just over half our support promised, Pastor Howard Holloway and I met for a prayer meeting. He said, "Flay, you're just wasting your time. The team needs you. Let's pray, set a date, and trust the Lord to provide the rest of your support."

We prayed and set the Puebla arrival date for six weeks later, February 26. Then pastor told me, "Don't worry about the expenses for the trip. My wife and I want to visit Mexico. We will drive down with you and take care of the expenses. You spend your money on the clothing and equipment that you will need."

In the following six weeks, churches and individuals promised enough support to bring the monthly support total up to $200.00. Because our trip costs were going to be covered, we used the extra money that came in through love offerings to buy clothing and a few household items that we would need.

On the Monday prior to our scheduled Friday departure date, pastor called me to tell me that his wife was sick and that they would not be able to go with us. "But," he added, "Don't worry. We'll come and visit you later."

Obviously he had forgotten that I was counting on him to pay for our trip to Mexico.

Since we had not saved money for the trip, I sat down and figured out the cost. Figuring costs for gas (at 30 cents per gallon), an oil change, food, and a one-night motel for $10.00, I came up with a total of $101.00 that we needed for the trip. Remember, this was Monday, and we were leaving on Friday.

We were not scheduled to speak anywhere on Wednesday night, so we prayed and decided to go to Flat Creek Baptist Church, a little country church outside of Fayetteville, Georgia. I hoped the pastor would ask me to preach, and then perhaps they would take a love offering for us. Arriving at the church, we discovered that they had invited another missionary to preach that night! Nevertheless, the pastor introduced us, told the congregation that we would be leaving for Mexico on Friday, and asked the people to pray for us. Before the other missionary preached, he asked Margaret and me to sing a duet.

After the service, a lady named Florine Adams came up to speak to me. When we shook hands, she gave me a folded bill and said, "My husband gave this to me before he died and told me to keep it for an emergency." Then she added, "I have a good job now, and I would like for you to use it on your trip to Mexico." I thanked her and put the bill in my pocket. We talked for a couple of minutes before she left. I then took the bill out and unfolded it. It was a $100.00 bill! That is big now, but it was huge in 1960.

I headed across the church to tell Margaret, and before I could say anything, she handed me a $1.00 bill that someone had given her. One hundred and one dollars! That's Philippians 4:19 again, *"But my God shall supply all your need according to His riches in glory by Christ Jesus."*

We left Atlanta on Friday with a song of praise in our hearts and arrived in Puebla on February 25th, one day ahead of schedule.

SIX
I'll Build Me a Desk

FOR OUR first term in Mexico, our house was filled with used furniture. I guess you would call our decor "Early Missionary." During the first year we put our milk, vegetables, etc. out on the window sill at night to try to keep them cool. After that year, we bought a used refrigerator for $75. Then we bought a used table and set of chairs. Margaret and I sanded and varnished them. They didn't really look like new, but we concluded that they did look less old.

Several in my family had construction abilities. My dad was a carpenter, and I even helped him build one house. My older brother, Bronner, could build anything. Out of scrap lumber, he built a gocart for us younger brothers, complete with steering wheel and brakes. Just for fun, he showed us how we could reverse the rope winding on the steering column causing it to go to the right when we turned it to the left, and vice-versa! We called his creation the Hunky Dunky. (For you older folks, it looked something like a 1949 Studebaker.)

Thinking I had inherited some of my dad's and brother's construction abilities, I decided to build a modern desk for my typewriter, complete with drawers for file folders.

However I didn't actually start from scratch. I found a table and started working on it and ended up with a desk with two nice big drawers and a small one.

I'm sorry that I never took a picture of the desk, but it did serve me well until we had to move to a different apartment. To my chagrin, I discovered that it would not go through the door. I tried the window, but the window was too small for my beautiful desk. I was forced to make a difficult decision—destroy the desk to get it out, or donate it to the landlord.

Now folks, I appreciate art, so I could not make myself deface a unique creation. If the old apartment building is still standing, some fortunate individual in Puebla, Mexico, has one of his bedrooms graced with an antique, hand-crafted, king-sized desk.

I had to tell Margaret, "Look, I'm a musician. You can't really expect me to also be a carpenter!"

SEVEN
Will This Motor Run,
or Will We Run?

SAN JOSE de Gracia (Saint Joseph of Grace) is a small village in southern Mexico, in the Oxajaca mountain range. When René Zapata, Earle Case, and I were there, the town had no electricity, no running water, and of course, no phone. Access to the village was not easy, but with some difficulty we managed to get to the remote area in Earle's pickup truck.

I guess we got off to a rough start. We distributed tracts the first day there, and a group of people got very much upset. They went to the mayor of the town and told him to get us out of their town with our strange doctrine, and that if he couldn't, they would.

The mayor met with us that afternoon to investigate. René explained that our purpose was to teach the Bible, God's Word, and to be a help to the community. Then he added, "We have heard that the motor for your corn grinder isn't running. A couple of the men in our team are mechanics." (A slight exaggeration, I would say.) René went on to say, "We would be happy to look at your motor and try to fix it." You see, without the motor, the ladies had to grind their corn by hand, using one smooth stone upon another.

The mayor met with the town council after our conversation, and they finally decided to let us see the motor early the next morning. We had our preaching service that evening, along with an urgent prayer meeting. We figured that either that motor was going to run, or we would run!

At 6:00 a.m., the mayor opened the shop door to let us see if we could repair the motor on the grinder which had only been installed a few months before under a government program for rural development. We were optimistic when we saw an almost new Briggs and Stratton engine. Our team had a standing rule that if there were people present that could not understand English, we would only speak in Spanish. But that day, we broke our rule. With the mayor and about four other men observing, we went to work. The instructions on the engine were printed in English, and we read them out loud. We meticulously cleaned everything that we could clean on the motor, and I would say that within five minutes we had discovered the problem. It was out of gas!

Well, it wasn't exactly that simple. The engine had a small gas tank for starting, and when it warmed up, could be switched to the larger main tank of kerosene. The main tank was not empty, but the motor would not start on kerosene. Earle went to his truck and siphoned enough gas to fill the little starter tank. During the 30 or 40 minutes we had been "repairing" the motor, the mayor and observers had not spoken a word. When the motor started, the mayor went into his office and brought each one of us a Pepsi which was hot, of course; but under the circumstances, it was delicious! We'd passed the test.

The evening meetings went well until the last day. On the final night, before we were ready to go up to the church building, the pastor called us to have a special prayer meeting. As he prayed, we noticed the urgency of his prayer. He was saying, "God, we're in Your hands. We want to please You. We want to serve You. But we are ready to meet You at any time; and if it's Your time to take us, we're ready to go. But we commit this situation into Your hands. We trust in You." He continued to pray like that. I must admit, I became pretty concerned.

I suppose the pastor thought our faith was so strong that it was not necessary to explain the situation to René, Earle, or me. He just said, "Ok, we men will go first, and we will take almost all of the lanterns; then 15 minutes later, the ladies can come."

Well, I'll admit that I was scared, but we started marching out across the field. When we got near the church, the pastor stopped by a corn field and said, "Ok, come on out!

We know you're in there." Six men came out of the corn field with machetes in their hands. The pastor said, "Look, we are here to preach the Gospel, and we're going to have our service as usual."

One of the men, the spokesman for the six, became quite vocal. He said that we were not going to go into the service and that we shouldn't be there. He continued stating that this is a Catholic town and that we were bringing in strange doctrine, and so on, and so forth.

At that point Earle Case, who was a big, tall fellow, especially compared to these little Mexican indigenous people, took over. With his booming bass voice, Earle said, "Ok, there's no time to talk now. We will talk about it after the service. It's time for our meetings to start now, and we're going to start on time." He put his arm around this little fellow and practically dragged him right toward the church and "ushered" him inside. The other five followed. Earle put them on the front row. He sat on the platform right in front of them and did not take his eyes off them during the entire service. Even during the prayer, Earle kept his eyes open and looked at each one of them. And those six men heard the glorious gospel of the Lord Jesus that night.

When the service was over, they forced one of the deacons to accompany them. One of the men had a pistol, and he threatened to kill the deacon if he would not buy them some Tequila. This brave deacon told him, "I don't drink Tequila now that I'm saved, and not only that, I'm not afraid to die. Go ahead and kill me." Well, that stunned them, and they finally let him go.

We found out later that these six men had gone to the mayor that same afternoon and had said, "Get these people out of town, or we'll do it our way."

The mayor answered, "No, they're here to teach the Bible, and they're friends of our community. They have fixed our motor and corn grinder, and we will cause them no harm." Then he sent a deputy to warn the pastor to be careful because these men might try to harm us.

One of the brethren discovered that they were hiding in a corn field and had warned the pastor.

Well the big surprise came early the next morning when we were to leave town. By 6:00 in the morning, the ladies had gotten up and barbequed a goat in our honor, because now they could have their corn ground in minutes, instead of spending hours doing it by hand. Not only did they have a barbequed goat, they gave us the delicacy of the head. Well, folks, I've eaten a lot of things on the mission field. But when I looked at that goat head, he was staring at me with his singed eyes. His teeth seemed to be laughing at me. I will have to say, it was a little difficult to carve around the nose for a few morsels of digestible meat. We didn't just "say grace," we asked for grace to be able to eat and enjoy what these local people considered a delicacy. They had given us their best. We will long remember it. And yes, we ate it with grateful hearts. God had protected us, and the Gospel had been preached in spite of the opposition of a few people who didn't want it to be heard.

EIGHT
24 Cents Worth of Gas

DURING OUR first year in Puebla, Mexico, I remember a particular time when we ran out of money. (This was not the only time; I just remember it as a *particular* time.) We had a commitment to be at a small church on the other side of Puebla for the Sunday morning service. From where we lived, there was no bus service. We had Margaret's nice Ford Fairlane, but the gas tank was almost on empty.

I started a careful search through all of our dresser drawers looking for nickels or pennies. Margaret joined in the search. I searched through all the pockets of my coats and pants. Between the two of us, we came up with a total (in pesos) of 24 cents!

There was a service station near our house. I told Margaret that we would get up early on Sunday morning, pray, go by the service station to buy gas, and drive until the car stopped. Then we would leave the car there and get our early morning exercise by walking the rest of the way to the church!

We pulled into the service station bright and early, and I hopped out of the car with a very cheery "BUENOS

DIAS." With a big smile, I told the attendant, "Put me in the big amount of 24 cents." He started pumping gas, and I started talking with him about what a beautiful day it was. Maybe I distracted him, or maybe he was just not in the habit of putting in such a small amount, but he didn't stop pumping at 24 cents, and I didn't stop talking at 24 cents.

All of a sudden he stopped and asked, "How much did you say?" I repeated, "24 cents." I don't remember the exact amount, but he had put in at least three times as much as I had ordered. I then explained to him that 24 cents really was all the money I had at the moment. But I told him that I lived close by, and I promised that in a few days, I would stop by and pay the balance. That seemed to satisfy him. I did stop by (as soon as I had the money) to pay him and give him a Gospel tract. With grateful hearts, Margaret and I drove all the way to church that morning and all the way back home after the service!

Anyway, Monday is a better day for early morning exercise.

NINE
The Ninety and Nine

EVEN THOUGH this story is about music, I want to start with preaching. The preaching of the Word of God is always first. God, in His wisdom, has chosen the foolishness of preaching in order that men might be saved. However, the right kind of Christ-honoring music runs a close second to preaching.

I am convinced that there is a lot of contemporary music in our churches that appeals to the flesh and is not Christ-honoring. I reject the idea that music is amoral. The contemporary Christian musicians use this argument in order to justify the use of rock music with Christian words in our worship services. Friends, instrumental music has a message! God used a harp, skillfully played, to bring healing to King Saul, and in this story God used a trombone skillfully played to bring salvation to souls. It is a case of preaching through music.

In 1961 our evangelistic team had a week of meetings in Tehuacán in a small Baptist church pastored by Felipe Lopez. Earle Case played a trombone solo of the well-known Gospel song, "The Ninety and Nine." Before playing he related the Gospel story. The first stanza told of the shepherd guiding and providing for his 100 sheep.

Then in the second stanza, Earle told how the shepherd discovered that one sheep was missing. The loving shepherd risked the dangers of darkness to frantically search for that one helpless animal. Then, of course, stanza three was a stanza of victory and rejoicing, because he found that poor lost sheep and lovingly carried it back in his arms to be safely joined to the fold.

When Earle finished relating the story, he played stanza one in a normal, pleasing style. But for the second stanza, which told of the search for that lost one, he switched to a slower tempo and a minor key. I still recall observing him as he played in that mournful minor tone with his eyes closed. But the third stanza was dramatically different. The tempo picked up. His tone vibrated brilliantly, and his stance, demeanor, and even the glow in his eyes, all came together in a victorious crescendo to keep the audience spellbound.

At that moment we all sensed God's presence in the audience. The sermon had already been preached. Earle had preached it on his trombone just as the sons of Asaph, Heman, and Jeduthun prophesied (preached) with harps, psalteries and cymbals. (I Chronicles 25:1) Evelio Perez gave the invitation, and as best as I can recall, two or three lost sheep came forward for salvation after Earle's trombone solo.

The right kind of music is a powerful means of getting out the Gospel message. In Psalm 40, David said "*He hath put a new song in my mouth, even praise unto our God: many shall see it, and fear, and shall trust in the Lord.*"

TEN
Scared Half to Death

WELL, WHO hasn't heard missionary stories of snakes, scorpions, and wild animals? And yes, I've heard the stories and have seen a few snakes and scorpions over the years, and I still don't claim to be exceptionally brave. They frighten me. I stay as far away from them as I can. But my most frightening experience did not involve serpents and wild animals.

From 1960 to 1963, our evangelistic team conducted campaigns in some of the most remote areas of Mexico. This frightening experience happened in a remote village, in the mountains, in the state of Puebla. Missionary Larry Puckett invited us for a campaign. He flew Earle Case, Evelio Perez, and me to his town in his small Cessna, named The Sparrow. There had been fierce opposition to the Gospel in the town, and Larry warned us that there could be serious trouble during the campaign.

The small village didn't have running water or electricity. But Larry had water. He dug a cistern on the side of the mountain at an elevation some 25 feet above his house, caught the rain water, and piped it into his house. (He also imported a lawn mower, an unknown piece of equipment in this town. The local people called it "the revolving machete.") Larry had built a tool shed on top of the cistern, and Earle, Evelio, and I slept there in sleeping bags.

The meetings went well for the first four days. We visited homes for several hours during the day and were exhausted by the time the evening meetings were over. The nights were usually cold and rainy, and the three of us would get dressed for bed and get into our sleeping bags; then each one of us would pray.

On Wednesday night, I was embarrassed because I had gone to sleep before it was my turn to pray. So Thursday night I was determined to keep my eyes open and stay awake. Earle prayed first, then Evelio. Now, Evelio prayed long prayers. It was raining. And as I lay there trying to keep my eyes open, I noticed a light flicker on the window. I imagined that the Puckett family had long since gone to bed, and it made me wonder if someone in the family might be sick. Then I saw a second light flicker. I got out of my sleeping bag and moved toward the window very quietly, so as not to disturb Evelio's praying, nor to wake Earle, (who, as I said, had already prayed).

Then I saw the lights. There were four or five men slowly approaching the missionary's home, with their lamps hidden behind them. I woke Earle and interrupted Evelio. By the time my coworkers got to the window, we could see more people with hidden lamps slowly approaching the house. We quickly concluded that they had come to kill the missionary. It dawned on us that we had no way of defending our fellow missionary or protecting ourselves. Larry had let us borrow his BB gun to shoot frogs that kept us awake at night, but we had nothing else. The crowd was growing. Evelio said, "Brothers, you watch, and I'll pray."

Then it happened! One of the men, right beside the bedroom window, whipped out his lighted torch, and in unison they all lifted their lamps. Evelio blurted out what the three of us were thinking at that moment, "They're going to burn the house down!" Humanly speaking, there seemed to be nothing that the three of us could do. In desperation, Evelio cried out, "God! Destroy them!"

Then, at that midnight hour, with our hearts racing and our hands trembling, we heard a unison outburst of voices as the crowd belted out, "Happy birthday to you!" in Spanish, of course!

We were mesmerized. None of us knew that it was Larry's birthday! We cried, we laughed, and we thanked God. We quickly got dressed and joined the church congregation as we all crowded into Larry's living room. We related to these dear brethren, who loved their pastor enough to come to his house on a cold rainy night and bring him a bit of cheer, how we had been totally convinced in our minds that their intention was to kill the missionary. We also told them how Evelio had cried out to the Lord saying "God, destroy them!"

For an hour and a half, we laughed, sang, gave testimonies, and prayed. A hearty shower of "Amens" came when one of the brethren exclaimed, "We certainly are grateful that God does not hear Evelio's prayers!"

ELEVEN
I Got Saved Last Year

MEXICO IS a big country with a high indigenous population. Our evangelistic team conducted meetings with four Indian groups: the Totonaco, the Zapoteca, the Misteca, and the Aztec. Missionary Loren Ediger scheduled us for meetings in a small Aztec village in the mountains of Puebla two years in a row. The Aztecs always seemed to be very warm and friendly. I still remember a few phrases in Aztec which they seemed to enjoy teaching us.

During our second visit to this particular village, the indigenous pastor and I entered the small one-room hut of an elderly man. He lived alone. When we walked in, he was squatting down in front of a pot of beans cooking on an open fire. He stood, a bit slowly, to receive us, and we entered into a lengthy conversation. He was short and obviously very old. He had all his front teeth, but I noticed that they were worn down almost to the gum.

After a bit, I asked him if he had trusted Christ as his Savior. With a surprised look on his face, he said, "Yes. I got saved when you were here last year. Don't you remember?" Well, I didn't remember.

I soon got up enough courage to ask him how old he was. He said that he wasn't exactly sure, but he asked us to come outside. He pointed out the cement block municipal building. (Just about all the other huts and buildings were made of adobe.) Then he told us, "That building was finished 96 years ago. I was a little boy about 5 or 6 years old and played on the sand pile while they were building it!"

That would put his age at 101 or 102 years old. And he was saved just one year earlier! He went on to tell us that he hadn't been able to attend the meetings this year in that his knees had started giving him problems. I could certainly understand. A little valley ran through town, and the church was on the hill opposite his hut. I was 27 at the time, and after a few hours of visitation up and down that mountain, my knees were giving me problems!

We saw a good harvest of souls that week, but none made me more happy than my newfound, old friend who "*as a firebrand plucked out of the burning*" was born again at the age of 100. (Amos 4:11)

I didn't remember from one year to the next when this Aztec gentleman had gotten saved, but he certainly remembered. Now, the important question is: Are you saved? You might not live to be 100!

TWELVE
Two For the Price of One

WE READ in Psalm 127:3 that "*children are an heritage of the Lord.*" God certainly blessed our home with three lovely daughters: Debbie, Becky, and Mimi. They were born during our first term of missionary service, while we were living in Puebla, Mexico.

When we discovered that Margaret was expecting Debbie, we were overjoyed with the prospect of soon becoming parents; but, I must confess, we were a bit concerned about our budget. We had no doubt that God would provide, but we sort of wondered how He would do it. Our support had been adequate, but we had to watch our spending very carefully.

We were fortunate to have Dr. Meadows, an elderly missionary doctor, attend Margaret during her pregnancy. She had excellent care. Debbie was born in the Latin American hospital in Puebla. The same week Debbie was born, we received a letter and check from a church in Atlanta that had never supported us. The check was for $75.00. When we went to the hospital to pay the bill, it was exactly $75.00!

God is faithful.

About a year later, Margaret visited Dr. Meadows again. He told her, "You're going to have a *very active baby*! I hear his heart on one side; then in no time he has turned, and I can hear the beat on the other side." (This was before the days of ultrasounds.) We had a boy's name chosen for this *very active baby* that was on the way.

Dr. Meadows was having some health issues, however, and he warned us that if our baby came at night he would not be able to deliver him. The hospital had just hired a young Mexican doctor, and Dr. Meadows suggested that we switch and start seeing him instead. (Actually, I think Margaret only saw the new doctor once before the day of delivery.)

A lady friend, Phyllis Raymond from Wisconsin, came to visit us when Margaret was in somewhat of an advanced stage. Margaret wanted to take her into town, and I said, "Okay, but it's time for you to see the doctor again. Go by the hospital first."

When the doctor examined her he said, "You're not leaving the hospital. This baby is coming!"

Phyllis didn't speak Spanish and hardly knew where we lived. Of course we had no phone. So Margaret wrote down our address and told Phyllis to get a taxi, show him the address, and get me to the hospital.

I arrived at the hospital, and 45 minutes later Mimi was born. The doctor thought his work was over until the nurse told him she thought she had discovered something. Five minutes later, Becky was born! The twins came as a total surprise. Margaret was fine, but I almost fainted! Two girls! When Margaret recovered, her first slurred comment was, "Three babies in fifteen months! I can't believe it!"

The next big surprise came when, that same week, we received a letter and check from the same church in Atlanta that had written us when Debbie was born. We had not heard from these folks in 15 months, but again, their letter came with a $75.00 check enclosed. When I went to pay the bill, they told me that since they didn't even know we were expecting twins, they would just give us two for the price of one—$75.00!

We've never heard from that church since. (Come to think of it, we've never had any more babies since either!) Margaret and I praise God for the three lovely ladies He's given us, and of course we praise Him for touching the heart of a pastor in Atlanta to supply our needs.

P.S. Folks, I must add a postscript. Several weeks after having written *Two for the Price of One*, Margaret and I received an inspiring letter from Sandy Payton, who reminded us that we had met in 1959 at Eastside Baptist Church in Atlanta. Eastside Baptist is the church that bought our babies! And I had forgotten the name of the church until I received Sandy's letter.

However, Margaret and I both remembered Sandy and her friend, Sara, from our two visits to Eastside. They were recent high school graduates, and Margaret and I, at age 25, had just started our deputation. At age 18, Sandy was already a very accomplished pianist. It was obvious that God had given her unusual musical talent. Each time we visited Eastside, we stayed after the service to listen to Sandy play hymn after hymn. We challenged her to dedicate her exceptional talent to the Lord and use it for His honor and glory.

Now let me quote from the surprise letter Margaret and I received from Sandy after all these years:

> *"Dear ones, Many years ago, having just graduated from high school I and my roommate, Sara Nealey, met you at Eastside Baptist Church. Your influence changed my life forever as I gave my heart fully to full-time Christian Ministry. . . . God has given me opportunity beyond my wildest dreams. I have*

traveled the globe. . . . I fell in love with missions all over the world, did a crusade in Sao Paulo, Brazil, and on and on—just a little mountain girl who has nothing to boast of in my own abilities, but I decided to keep my life clean and ask God to use me. I have shared a few events to let you know that the legacy that you have planted just keeps on going . . . all because two young [people] 'in love with each other and Jesus' walked into my life, my heart, and I carried you with me all the way." I love you, Sandy Payton.

Thanks, Sandy, for your edifying letter.

CHILE

THIRTEEN
A Friendly Yankee in Wisconsin

AFTER COMPLETING our first term of missionary service, our team was invited and encouraged to transfer to Chile for our second term. After praying about it, we decided to make the move. However, we discovered that the cost of living was much higher in Chile than in Mexico and found it necessary to raise additional support before making the move."

With that in mind, a pastor friend scheduled me for deputation meetings in Wisconsin. Can you believe that he scheduled the meetings for the middle of winter! Now I'm from the Deep South and had never been to the North Pole before. Margaret wasn't able to accompany me since this would have been a long trip with our three daughters in the winter.

Fortunately, I talked with my good friend David Robinson. (David and Betty have been long time friends and supporters.) David was a military man and had traveled a lot more than I had. He advised me not to head to Wisconsin in the dead of winter without snow tires on my station wagon. Then he added, "My sister-in-law has two snow tires she will be glad to give you if you will come to Belmont, North Carolina, so we can mount them." The tires were in the crawl space under her house and looked good, but who knows how long they had been there. We mounted them.

I was invited to speak at a youth rally on Saturday night at Garfield Baptist Church in Milwaukee. Ernie and Shirley Cochran, former BJU students, were members of Garfield Baptist, so they decided to attend the youth rally and meet me.

Now I was somewhat of a stranger in Yankee land. Wisconsin was the farthest north I had ever traveled. (In 1965, I was not very far removed from my Carolina farm days.) My Southern accent always gave me away. Even though I was a bit nervous, I managed to get started by saying, "I am really proud to be here with you all tonight. I can already see that I was wrong about you all. I have always heard that Yankees are not very friendly. Well, you folks are friendly tonight. And even on my way here, just a few miles out of town, a well-dressed gentleman stopped and wanted to talk with me. He wanted to know where I was coming from, and where I was going. He looked at my station wagon and even wanted to see what a South Carolina driver's license looked like." The friendly people laughed, and I guess that helped me to get over my nervousness. So I further explained that the man had stopped because one of my snow tires had blown out! The kind policeman helped me put on the spare tire.

When the rally was over, Ernie and Shirley came up to talk with me. We had a long, friendly chat before they left. Ernie drove out of the parking lot, but then said to Shirley, "Let's go see what kind of car the missionary is driving." They came back into the parking lot, found my station wagon, and saw that I had another flat tire! When they came in and told the pastor, he called a service station and had them come out and put on two new tires.

Since it was already late on Saturday night, all the folks went home except Ernie, who waited with me until the station wagon was ready. We had a long time to talk. Ernie had a lot of questions about our ministry. Then before leaving, he took out two credit cards and told me, "put all of your gas on these cards until your deputation is over and you are ready to go to Chile!" I had never used a credit card before; I am not sure I had even seen one. But it reminded me of Jeremiah 33:3, and I considered it just one more of those tremendous surprises that God wants to show us.

Margaret and I soon formed a great love and appreciation for Ernie and Shirley. We became very close friends. The stereotype I had of Yankees not being friendly was quickly disappearing. Seven years later, Shirley flew to Spain to play the piano for our first LP recording. I guess it just reminded me that, Yankee or Rebel, "*A man that hath friends must show himself friendly,*" and that I should never forget that Jesus "*is a friend that sticketh closer than a brother,*" Proverbs 18:24.

FOURTEEN
A Hike Over the Andes

A CLOSE-UP view of the majestic towering peaks of the Andes Mountains is an awesome, unforgettable sight. I have been privileged to see the Canadian Rockies, as well as the Swiss Alps. But after Margaret and I, with our three daughters, lived for four years in Santiago, Chile, with a daily breathtaking view of the snow-covered peaks of the Andes from our back yard, I'm partial. I have crossed them by plane, car, train (an option that no longer exists), and on foot.

In July, 1964, in the middle of the South American winter, Carey Clark and I made a brief survey trip to Argentina. We traveled by bus from Santiago to Puerto Montt. (The famed Pan-American Highway, which extends from Alaska through the Yukon, Canada, the States, as well as Central and South America, ends at the dock in Puerto Montt.) There we took a different bus toward Argentina to the road's end, at the beginning of the huge Llanquihue Lake.

While waiting for the ferry, which would take us across the lake and to the foothills of the Andes, we met Hamilton and Ingrid—a lovely, unforgettable couple. Hamilton was a doctor who worked for NASA training chimpanzees for possible space flights. Remember, this is 1964, five years before we put a man on the moon. Hamilton was very enthusiastic as he talked to us about his prized student, an astute monkey named "Ham." Sadly, our acquaintance was short lived. We witnessed to them and gave them a Gospel tract, but the call to board the ferry came all too soon. Seeing that they were good humored, as we boarded I told Hamilton that I would think about him when I heard that NASA had put a monkey on the moon!

Llanquihue is an enormous lake, 30 miles wide at one point, and is strategically surrounded by mountains and forests. It offers a breathtaking view of Patagonia's 8,500-foot snow-capped volcano, Mount Osorno. After sailing by miles and miles of pristine vegetation which would have been a challenge for Zane Grey to adequately describe, we disembarked and almost immediately boarded the rustic-looking bus which was to take us over the Andes and into Argentina. Through a heroic effort, the bus managed to climb what I would have estimated to be four or five thousand feet of winding highway. A fresh snow of four to six inches had fallen during the predawn hours, and we were forced to park at a pre-designated area and wait for a Caterpillar tractor to tow us up the last steep climb.

One of us (I believe it was Carey) had the wild idea for the two of us to start hiking and see how far and how high we could get before we got bogged down in the snow drifts. At that point we would simply wait for the tractor and bus. Most of the passengers were local people and thought we were two "crazy Yankees" to want to hike on ahead of the bus. But the bus driver said, "Adelante." (Go ahead.)

At least I can say that we were properly dressed for the hike. We both wore boots, gloves, overcoats, and caps. Almost immediately we noticed animal tracks leading up the road ahead of us. A couple of times they disappeared in the woods for a few feet, but always came back to the road. Neither of us was a hunter, and we knew absolutely nothing of South American wildlife. I was hoping to see a deer by the time we reached the top, but we only saw tracks. We kept climbing, and the snow got deeper. Finally, exhausted and half frozen, we saw the sign "Bienvenido a Argentina" (Welcome to Argentina). I still have a picture of the welcome sign.

The Aduana station was a few hundred feet on down the Argentine side. (Chile and Argentina continue to argue about the exact national border lines in the southern part of the countries. That might be why the official entry station had this slight offset.) Carey and I were still congratulating ourselves on our successful climb to the top of the Andes and admiring the panoramic view when we heard the tractor. That gave us the additional adrenalin to trudge on toward the Aduana checkpoint. We actually arrived at the border checkpoint about five minutes ahead of the bus!

Everyone on the bus congratulated us, but then started asking if we weren't scared. We told them, "no." Then they asked, "But didn't you see those mountain lion tracks?" We told them that yes, we saw them, but weren't scared.

Crazy Yankees!

FIFTEEN
A 24-Day Cruise

A FEW days ago I received an exciting telemarketing call informing me that I had won two free tickets for a five-day cruise to the Bahamas! Wow! All I had to do was fill out a brief survey. Incredible! How could I be so fortunate? Two free tickets!

Now really, folks. I was born at night, but I was not born last night! There had to be a catch to it. So I firmly refused the temptation to bite. Nevertheless, it has been hard for me to get my mind off the Bahamas—tropical summer weather, breath-taking landscapes, turquoise water, exotic sounds (and smells?). When I finally forced myself to come back to reality, it dawned on me that a five-day cruise to the Bahamas would pale by comparison to the Allen family 24-day "cruise" from New Orleans to Viña del Mar, Chile.

When Margaret and I were preparing for our trip to Santiago, Chile, for our second term of missionary service, we were advised to take a refrigerator and washing machine plus a few other basic items. We checked ticket prices on all the airlines for us to fly, but we would still need to make arrangements to send the appliances some other way.

Then we made a wonderful discovery! The cargo ships to Chile were permitted to accommodate up to 12 passengers without having a doctor on board. After checking the sea fares, we realized that it would actually be more economical for *us* to go by freighter than to fly, since the ticket price included several square feet of luggage. So we immediately booked passage on the USS Gulf Shipper.

Cruising from New Orleans through the Gulf of Mexico turned out to be the longest leg of our voyage, especially when you take into account that four out of the five of us (names withheld) were suffering bouts of sea sickness. As you can imagine, the dock in Panama was a welcome sight.

While waiting for the loading and unloading of cargo, we found three or four boys fishing. They had only a string, a hook, and a can of worms. Debbie, Becky, and Mimi were very small then but were fascinated by seeing the boys pull up little minnows on a string. Our three wanted to fish! I convinced one boy to sell me his string and hook for about 50 cents, plus 10 cents each for three worms. So our daughters had their first fishing trip to Panama!

I had read about the challenges and difficulties the Americans faced in building the famous Panama Canal and that many had lost their lives to malaria and yellow fever while working on the project. So it was fascinating to see firsthand this marvelous feat of engineering and construction and observe how the canal locks worked to raise the ship three levels then lower it again as we approached the Pacific. (I still think President Carter made a serious mistake by giving it away.)

At Buenaventura, Colombia, we had an eight-hour stop-over. Our family welcomed the opportunity to go ashore and do a bit of "window-shopping." Our most vivid memory came from our little "tea party." A Colombian lady was working on her balcony when she saw the five of us walk by hand in hand. She called out, "Are you Americans?" When we responded in the affirmative, she invited us into her house for tea and cookies. We had more than an hour to explain to her the purpose of our trip to Chile and to explain the Gospel message. We spent a very pleasant afternoon with our newfound friend at our first South American Tea Party!

On our voyage, the Gulf Shipper had a crew of 44. In addition to our family of five, there were two other passengers on the ship. We had our meals with the officials—namely the Captain, and the first, second, and third mates. The Captain seemed to take quite an interest in our trip. He gave us kitchen and refrigerator privileges 24/7. (I'll bet that would never happen on a cruise to the Bahamas!)

We formed a strong friendship with the third mate, Dick Rahn, which lasted until his home going some 10 years ago. Dick was a typical church attendee but had no idea if he was saved. We met several times to study the Bible and pray. Praise the Lord, by the time we arrived in Chile, he was sure that he was a born-again Christian.

The Captain gave me permission to hold a Sunday morning service the last two Sundays we were on the ship. Our family sang some hymns accompanied by my new accordion-organ, and I preached. Almost all of the crew attended both Sundays and heard a Gospel message each week. Other than Dick Rahn's salvation, we didn't see any visible results, but we claimed Romans 10:17: *"So then faith cometh by hearing and hearing by the word of God."*

At some magic unmarked point in the vast Pacific, the Captain called our family together and presented each one of us with an official signed document stating that we had sailed across the Equator.

We arrived at Callao, Peru, on a Saturday, and the ship docked there until Monday. I had the address of some missionaries in Lima, so we took a bus in and spent Saturday night with them. On Sunday, they invited Margaret and me to sing; then I preached in the morning service. On Sunday afternoon we took a bus back to the ship.

As often as possible, I tried to spend time on deck with my newfound brother, Dick Rahn. On one of those occasions,

I experienced a splendid Kodak moment. Out in the enormous ocean on a sunny afternoon, a brief shower brought a refreshing breeze. All of a sudden, there appeared the most beautiful and most complete rainbow I had ever observed. It seemed that we could almost visualize a complete circle as the brilliant colors rose up from the emerald blue waters into a near cloudless sky then arched unbroken into the water on the other side. This one breathtaking moment transported me back some 4,500 years to the moment when God spread out the first celestial rainbow before the eyes of His servant, Noah. God enveloped in that rainbow a special promise for His faithful servant. As I observed that South American rainbow, I was reminded that God has given us a multitude of promises in His Word to strengthen our weak faith. We were on our way to the mission field, and the promise that came to my mind was Matthew 28:20: *"And lo, I am with you alway, even unto the end of the world."* We certainly felt His presence.

Our 24-day cruise finally came to an end in the colorful coastal city of Viña del Mar, Chile. We had cruised through the Gulf of Mexico and the Panama Canal. We had experienced a Fishing Trip and a Tea Party. We received an Equator Certificate and had seen a brilliant Rainbow of Promise. Most importantly, a precious soul had been saved.

Now who is interested in the Bahamas anyway?

SIXTEEN
New Life

WHILE LIVING in Santiago, Chile, three of my coworkers and I formed a team with the plan of going into Las Condes, one of the more affluent sections of the city, to start an Independent Baptist Church. We went two by two and door to door. We gave a copy of the Gospel of John to each family. Most families received us well, and we tried to take every opportunity to present the plan of salvation.

In this upper class section of the city, we were usually received by the maid. But during our first week of visitation in the area, I knocked on a door, and a banker named Gustavo Olivares came to the door. I gave him a Gospel of John and told him that if he had time I would like to talk with him about the central theme of the Bible.

Gustavo invited us in, and for the next two hours we answered his questions and explained the plan of salvation. He had studied with two or three cults without finding the answers to his questions and, to the contrary, had become more confused. But God opened his heart that day, and I realized he was asking the right questions. He seemed to understand his own condition and need.

Finally I asked him, "Gustavo, do you want to receive Christ as your personal Savior?"

"Yes," he responded.

Then I asked, "When?"

"Right now!"

So I told him we would get on our knees and pray, and I said, "You pray first, and then I'll pray."

Gustavo told me that he had memorized and recited prayers, but that he did not know how to pray spontaneously. So I just said to him, "Gustavo, you have told me about your desire to know God. You have told me of your failures and disappointments. You've told me you want God to forgive you of your sin and be your Savior. Now just talk directly to God and tell Him what you have told me."

Well, he started. It was such a thrill to hear Gustavo pray in such a natural way. He just said "God, for a long time I have wanted to get my life straightened out with You but didn't know what to do. Now You have let these two men come today to talk to me, and they have told me that there is nothing that I can do anyway, that Jesus has already done it all. So I want You to forgive me of my sins. I want

Jesus to be my Savior." He continued praying and praying and praying for a long while.

Finally I realized that I had told him how to *start* his prayer, but I hadn't told him how to *end* it! Gustavo wanted to do everything right, so he finally closed his prayer just as if he were finishing a letter to God. He just said, "Lord, without anything further for this afternoon, I remain, your most sincere friend and servant, Gustavo Olivares."

Then I prayed, and when we got up, he had tears in his eyes and gave me a big bear hug. He was thrilled about having found new life—spiritual life in Christ. He even asked me to give him a list of things that he should or shouldn't do now that he was a Christian. I told him that I wouldn't give him a list, but that the Holy Spirit, which now dwelt within him, would teach him. I did make four suggestions though:

- Read your Bible every day. God talks to you through His Word.
- Pray every day. That is how you talk to God.
- Come to all of our Bible studies, and you will learn about the Christian life.
- Start telling your friends that you have accepted Christ and that He has saved you.

Within just a few weeks, his wife and two others in his family got saved.

After having been saved only a month, Gustavo came to me one afternoon with a poem he had written. He said, "I am trying to express in poetry the joy that I have now that I have accepted Christ as my Savior. The title of the poem was *NEW LIFE*. I read the poem and was thrilled. I took the poem home and wrote the music for it that very night. Sometime later Dr. Frank Garlock published it under Majesty Music in the Praises I hymnbook. The words to the chorus are:

> *Oh what delight fills my heart,*
> *For He is all to me.*
> *How can I help but sing His praise?*
> *Jesus has set me free!*

Have you experienced that new life in Christ? If not, follow Gustavo's example. If you will call on Jesus by faith, He will save you. Just talk to God!

SEVENTEEN
Sing It Again

IN MY younger days, I always sang tenor. For the Music Education degree, I had a voice proficiency and was required to give a vocal recital in order to graduate. My voice teacher classified my voice as a lyric tenor but would not permit me to sing higher than a "G." He was concerned that I would hurt my voice.

Margaret and I were in our early 30s when we arrived in Santiago. We were doing a lot of singing in those days. I was teaching voice and directing the choir in our Bible Institute. We discovered that we could sign up for voice class at the Santiago Conservatory almost free of charge. It was a great opportunity for us to grow with the ministry, and it opened the door to a class of people that we possibly could not have otherwise reached with the Gospel.

Our voice teacher was Miss Inez Carmona. She was an opera singer with a powerful contralto voice. She was also an active Communist. She belonged to the upper echelon group and was a personal friend of Salvador Allende and the famous poet, Pablo Neruda.

We witnessed to Miss Carmona from the very beginning. We gave her a Bible and a book on the persecuted underground church in Russia.

Actually, we became good friends. She invited us into her home on more than one occasion and helped us learn the songs assigned to us in voice class. Margaret and I learned the soprano-tenor duet, Libiamo, from La Traviata, by Giuseppe Verdi. The duet ends with a high "B flat" sung in unison. (Now remember, my former voice instructor had forbidden me to sing higher than a "G.")

When we learned the music, we went to Miss Carmona's home to practice. Since I am a piano tuner, I noticed right away that her piano was about a step flat. But even at that, when we sang Libiamo, I didn't sing the high note at the end. I sang a lower note in harmony with Margaret. Miss Carmona instructed us to sing it again, and sing the high note. Well, since I knew that the piano was flat, and that in reality, I would only be singing an "A flat," I thought that maybe just a half step higher than my limit wouldn't hurt. So, I sang it.

The following week, we had our final exam at the conservatory and had to sing before a panel of three music professors. When our time came, Margaret and I smiled and sang Libiamo. Unfortunately, the conservatory piano was in tune! So, when we ended the duet, I sang a lower harmony note—a "D" to be exact. The students applauded, and I was still smiling when I received a powerful surprise. Miss Carmona had been seated on the platform behind me with the others on the panel. All of a sudden, she gave me a powerful sideways kick in the seat of the pants, which almost knocked me off the platform, and yelled "Sing it again!"

We had to repeat the song. This time I wasn't as concerned about hurting my voice as I was hurting my anatomy. We repeated the duet, and as I contemplated the real possibility of having bodily harm inflicted on the posterior of my anatomy, I didn't just sing a high "B flat"; I belted out a Ray Gibbs high "B flat"! (Some 10 years later in Spain, under the direction of voice professor Dolores Perez, in the Verdi Requiem, I actually sang a high "B natural." I believe even Inez Carmona would have gotten a kick out of that.)

The last time we saw Miss Carmona and told her we were leaving Chile, she cried. She told me that she was confused, and that even the Communist Party leaders had threatened to discipline her because she was wavering. When I returned to Chile for a campaign 18 years later, I tried unsuccessfully to locate her. We have prayed for her. We can only rest in the fact that we thoroughly explained to her that God does exist and that someday she will have to stand before Him to give an account of her brief life here. We explained to her that we are all sinners but that Christ died to pay the price for our sin, and that if we repent, confess our sin and trust Jesus, He will forgive us and save us.

We hope that she did accept Christ's payment for her sin so that we can see her again one day in heaven.

SPAIN

EIGHTEEN

That's My Uncle Who is a Missionary in Spain

TRANSPORTATION CAN sometimes be a challenge for the missionary. During our four-year term in Burgos, Northern Spain, we lived four miles out of the city in a quaint village called Quintanadueñas. Our twin daughters had scoliosis, a very noticeable lateral curvature of the spine. The doctors recommended swimming as the best exercise prior to possible surgery. Margaret needed our car to take the three daughters to a military sports club, where they had a heated swimming pool. We couldn't afford two cars, so I bought a used Montesa motorcycle to ride into Burgos each day to meet my coworker, Dennis Flower, for tract distribution and visitation.

Now a Montesa, 175 cc, was not a fancy bike. It didn't have any chrome on it but was acceptable transportation. However, a year later, a missionary friend of mine, Brother Eddie Woodfield, offered to sell me his Bultaco. Now the Bultaco *Metralla* (machine gun) was a motorcycle! I remembered that in the 1960s when we were in Santiago, the Chilean motor-cross champion rode a Bultaco. I was getting the fever. (It just could be that this bike thing runs in the family. When Andy Bonikowsky was 18, he rode his 49cc motor bike 750 miles, from Irún, Northern Spain, to visit us in Elche, Southern Spain. He made the trip non-stop in 22 hours! As best I recall, he was learning to tune pianos at the time and wanted me to give him some pointers. But, come to think of it, he and our daughter, Mimi, had been communicating as "just friends" for about four years already.)

But one cold, misty night, the Bultaco let me down. I had to go into Burgos to take an urgent message to our school teacher. It was drizzling rain. I thought it would be the perfect night to try out my new waterproof rubberized rain suit, so I rode the Bultaco. Visibility was so poor that I was only going about 20 miles per hour. All of a sudden, the bike slipped out from under me. As I was sliding on my back, I sensed some kind of resistance. In fact, I was instantly bombarded by repugnant malodorous fumes. I soon discovered the cause.

A tractor, pulling a trailer loaded with soupy manure had gone ahead of me. At the point where I fell, the tailgate of the trailer had come open and dumped a foot of the stinking stuff on the road. It took me a week to get rid of the smell on my clothing and motorcycle. (Ruth Ann Flower said it was a good thing I had on my rubber pants!)

But that letdown didn't stop me from riding. When we came for our next furlough, we visited our dear friends David and Betty Robinson. Their son, Davy, had a

Harley-Davidson Sportster. It was a Chopper with the extended forks, raised handlebars and chrome all over! Now, that was a motorcycle to make even my riding friend, Bob Miller, jealous. (Bob had two dirt bikes, and on earlier furloughs, he and I would go riding.)

One day when I was admiring Davy's Harley, he said, "Why don't you take my Sportster someday and ride up to North Carolina to visit your Dad. Now that was an excellent idea. So, one sunny September afternoon, dressed in Levi's, boots, Davy's Army field jacket, gloves, and a dark shielded helmet, I headed to North Carolina.

At the same moment I arrived at my Dad's house out in the country, the county school bus stopped to let my nephew, Phil Allen, off. The driver asked Phil, "Who in the world is that?" Phil told him, "I think that is my uncle who is a missionary in Spain." The bus driver responded immediately, "That is *not* your uncle who is a missionary in Spain!"

Well, I'm older now. I think the fever has left me. Nevertheless, if you hear someday that Bob Miller and I are looking for two used Bultaco wheel chairs (with chrome wheels), don't be surprised.

NINETEEN
Don't Worry: He'll Come Back

MARGARET AND I arrived in Spain in January, 1971. While waiting for two other families of our team to arrive, we worked with missionaries Jim and Carol West.

As soon as we got somewhat settled in our apartment, Jim took me to his barber for a haircut in a lovely downtown Madrid area, right beside the picturesque Plaza Castilla. Jim got his hair cut first and then left me with his barber while he went shopping. After my haircut, I settled down to wait for Jim.

Credit where credit is due: I must say that under General Franco's dictatorship, the blatant pornography and sordid literature, which is now so prevalent in Spain, was not tolerated. At that time, the reading material available in waiting rooms was generally very wholesome.

I picked up an illustrated storybook and began to read. The story turned out to be rather dramatic, well written, and quite sad. Before long, I had tears in my eyes. (I admit I tend to be quite emotional.) Jim delayed his return, and I kept reading. Pretty soon, tears were running down my cheeks. (Here I am, a 37-year-old man with tears running down my cheeks like a baby.)

I didn't realize anyone was observing me until the barber came over and patted me on the shoulder. With a grandfatherly tone of voice he said, "Don't worry. Jim will come back for you."

I was too choked up and embarrassed to try to explain that I was teary eyed because of the tragedy in the story. All I managed to do was nod and mumble a feeble "thank you," while continuing to read my sad story!

TWENTY

If the Son Therefore Shall Make You Free

CARLOS WAS young and talented. He had a slim athletic build and was a gifted baseball player. But, Carlos was Cuban. His dream of being a professional baseball player seemed to be cut short when he was drafted into Castro's army, but Carlos was stubborn and determined. In fact, he was determined to leave Cuba and find freedom no matter what the cost.

Carlos came up with a plan of escape. It was very complex with several weaknesses. He probably had less than a 5% chance of succeeding, but he was willing to risk all in an effort to escape. He was serving in the military in Havana, and the first step in his plan was a self-inflicted "accidental" pistol shot in the leg which put him in the military hospital.

Then in a daring effort, he took the second step. Within less than 48 hours, he made his escape from the hospital and went into hiding.

His third step called for the necessary physical training required to accomplish his complicated plan. He found refuge with a friend who lived near the beach and started his training as soon as his leg was sufficiently healed. Every day (or night) he would swim for hours.

Carlos had a friend who worked on a Greek cargo ship. Through the limited means of communication that was available at that time, and over a period of two years, Carlos and his friend worked on the most complicated and dangerous part of his plan—his escape from the closely-guarded island. They set the date (night, of course) when the cargo ship would pick him up four miles off the Cuban coast in the Atlantic!

When my family traveled on the cargo ship from New Orleans to Chile, it took 24 days. However, Dick Rahn (the third mate) told us that the same voyage three months earlier had taken 28 days. Because of bad weather, we almost had to bypass Viña del Mar, our port of entry, to go on to Puerto Montt. We would have returned to our destination a week later. Imagine how complicated it would be for a cargo ship to meet an exact schedule, sailing from Europe past the shores of Havana!

Another major weakness in the plan was that the waters around the Cuban coasts are shark infested. Some say there is no danger of sharks if there is no blood, but I am not too sure about that. In 1957 when I had the privilege of traveling with an evangelistic team throughout the island, we had two weeks of camp with missionary Roy Ackerle in

Cabañas, Pinar del Río. Roy had a small motorboat and I actually learned to water ski that summer in the Cabañas bay. Roy warned my coworker and me not to go far out from shore and that if anyone fell, to get them in the boat immediately. Years later, Roy told me about taking some men fishing just two miles off the Havana coast. One of the men hooked a big one which fought him almost all of the way to the boat. Then, all of a sudden it gave up, and he pulled in half of a huge fish. A shark had a nutritious breakfast with the other half.

After two years of training, Carlos knew how long it would take him to swim the four miles. He also knew that, if the weather cooperated, he could tread water or float for hours.

I believe God was watching over every detail. On the appointed night, Carlos reached the estimated four-mile point of rendezvous ahead of schedule. The ship was almost on schedule. The captain and crew spotted Carlos just before daylight. Carlos, practically exhausted and running on adrenaline, was taken on board for a joyful reunion with his faithful friend. He had obtained his goal of freeing himself from the strangling grip of communism! He was a free man.

A few weeks later the captain dropped Carlos off at the port in San Sebastian, Spain. From there, he made his way to Madrid. I met Carlos and heard his thrilling story in 1971 while on visitation with missionary Jim West. Carlos was living with two other Cuban refugee families in a small downtown apartment.

But that night, Carlos told us the rest of the story. In Spain, he had heard the glorious message of salvation. Carlos had accepted Christ by faith, and the chains of sin which had bound him had also been broken. He had finally found real freedom. I could only think of John 8:36: "*If the son therefore shall make you free, ye shall be free indeed.*"

TWENTY-ONE
May I Make a Suggestion?

OUR MISSIONARY team recorded our first two LP albums (33 RPM) while we were planting a church in the province of Burgos, in northern Spain. Even if we were a bit limited with what we could do with our voices, we always strived for a good variety in the accompaniment. I had played the double bass (or string bass, as it is commonly called) in the orchestra at BJU for a couple of years. I just loved the depth that it added to a recording. String basses were expensive in Spain, but with the help of an instrument repair friend in Madrid, I was able to trade my viola for a string bass.

Dennis Flower and I drove to Madrid to pick it up in a Mini Morris. Now the Mini Morris (or Austin Mini here in the United States) is a very fine but very small car. My instrument repair friend lived in old downtown Madrid, just about three blocks from the famous Atocha Train Station. (Why didn't we think of going by train?)

We parked the Mini in front of my friend's house on a narrow, but rather busy street. We brought the string bass out to the sidewalk and discovered that it was taller than we were! We opened all four doors of the Mini and turned the seats down; but after a few attempts, we had failed to get the bass inside the car.

A small crowd was gathering, and we were sweating. An elderly gentleman, well-dressed with suit and tie as was the custom in Madrid in 1972, was observing our futile attempts at putting the instrument in. Finally he asked, "May I make a suggestion?" By that time we were ready to listen to any suggestions from anyone. Then he said, "Why don't you just put the car inside the bass?"

Well, to make a long story short, we finally did get the bass to Burgos, but don't ask me how!

TWENTY-TWO
A More Meaningful Religious Experience

D URING THE 1970s, camping was big in Europe. In those days, it was considered a safe and inexpensive way to take a vacation. I will admit that our family seldom took a bona fide vacation. If we had a visiting pastor, we showed him different ministries around Spain. That was a vacation (especially if he took care of the expenses).

But in 1972 we did take a bona fide business vacation. Margaret needed an accordion. Before leaving Chile we had sold her accordion thinking they would be less expensive in Spain. But we were wrong. After checking several music stores and seeing the prices of accordions, we came up with a brilliant idea. Before going to Chile, I had taught accordion and had also ordered and sold a few. Through a friend, I had made contact with an accordion manufacturer in Italy.

So, we decided to use a camping tent, take a two-week business vacation, and drive to Italy to buy Margaret a new accordion. It turned out to be a fascinating and rewarding trip. I will only highlight three of the most memorable events that took place.

In Béziers, France, driving near the Riviera, we could sense that a storm was blowing in. We found a camping place as soon as possible and asked for a spot to erect our tent. The manager saw our family and our need. He said, "We are full, and normally I would just say 'no.' But a storm is coming in. Find any spot you can that is big enough for your tent, and I suggest that you hurry."

We quickly pitched tent and had it securely staked down by the time the strong wind and rain started. It was a miserable night that I don't think Margaret nor I will ever forget. We slept little and prayed lots. The tent held, but the wind blew the aluminum frame out of shape. It was still usable, but from then on, it got a lot of attention. To use a North Carolina term, it was noticeably lopsided after the storm until we finally got rid of it several years later.

The next event was enjoyable and rewarding. It took place in Foligno, Italy. When we checked in to the camping place, I showed my residence card for identification. The attendant said, "Your people are over there in that direction," and she pointed west.

Now we didn't know a soul in Italy, but I am a curious person, so I headed west. Pretty soon, we found "our people." There was a group of perhaps 40 Christians singing hymns and getting ready to eat. We told them who we were as best we could (Spanish-English-Italian-sign language), and they invited us to join them for supper. (I understood that.) It turned out to be a church group that was having a three-week tent campaign with the plan of planting a church in Foligno.

After eating, I got Margaret, Debbie, Becky, and Mimi bedded down (in sleeping bags and on air mattresses in our lopsided tent) and then I accompanied "our people" to the tent meeting. Eight people had already gotten saved, and I am convinced that, by the time the three weeks of meetings were over, they would be able to plant a church. It dawned on me that the attendant had sent me west to meet "my people" because I had listed on my residence permit "Baptist Pastor" as my profession.

The third and most important event took place in France on our return trip. Since I don't speak French, I had followed the signs to a seasonal camping site. Well, camp season was over. The gates were still open, and the facilities were functioning but only a handful of people were scattered around. While we were considering what to do, a young couple drove up and asked if we spoke English. We had a brief conversation and were very positively impressed with them. They were newlyweds from New York City named Frank and Debbie. We decided that we would erect our tents close together and keep an eye out for each other.

The next morning we were preparing breakfast when Frank and Debbie crawled out of their tiny tent. Margaret said, "Let's invite them for breakfast." I did, and they accepted. We had only packed two cups (and three glasses) for our trip, one for Margaret and one for me. But we shared. Margaret and I used one cup, and Frank and Debbie used the other. They were both artists. Frank had just received his Master's from Yale, and Debbie had earned her Master's at Davis Art Institute.

Conversation came easily. They both came from a Catholic background and had never met a missionary before. Frank told me that one of the decisions they had made when they got married was "to find a more meaningful religious experience." Wow! By then our schedule was tight and so was theirs, but we gave them our address in Burgos and invited them to come and visit us. We gave them tracts and finally had to say goodbye and head for home.

About four days later, Frank and Debbie drove up. It was just like meeting old friends. We started explaining the plan of salvation from the day they arrived, and both showed a vital interest. I explained to them that our God is a Holy God and cannot have fellowship with us because of our sin. But that He loved us so much that He made a way for sins to be forgiven. He sent His only son, Jesus, who had never sinned, to the cross of Calvary to pay the penalty of our sins. I explained Romans 5:8 to them, that God's love was so great that, in spite of our sin and rejection of Him, He gave His son in our place. And I explained to Frank that they didn't need a religious experience, but rather a new life. They needed forgiveness and salvation through Christ.

Their hearts were open. They had never really heard the Gospel story. Frank kept saying, "It is all so logical."

On their second night with us, they went to their room, got on their knees and asked the Lord to save them. The next morning, Margaret and I were in the kitchen when Debbie walked in. With a big smile on her face she said, "We did it."

I asked, "Did what, Debbie?"

She said, "We accepted Christ."

That left us two days for discipleship classes. Early on the morning after the fourth day, we hugged and said goodbye.

While we were eating supper that night, they drove up again! They had left their passports in our kitchen on a window stand. We had two more days of follow-up classes!

We have since visited them three times in New York. Now they live in Pennsylvania, and we hope to visit them again sometime.

And what about the accordion? The best price we found in Spain was $450.00. We bought a new one at the factory for $165.00. What a vacation! We had weathered a raging storm, witnessed the process of a church plant, and two souls accepted Christ.

A "religious experience" won't get anyone to heaven. Jesus said, "*I am the way, the truth and the life. No man cometh to the Father but by me.*" John 14:6

TWENTY-THREE
I Want the Evidence On You

L OCATED RIGHT in the center of the city of Burgos is a beautiful promenade, called the Espolón. This colorful walkway seems to have a magnetic attraction in summertime. It is a favorite hangout for young people and a popular gathering place for the entire family.

It was summer in 1972 when our newly-formed church decided to go to the Espolón on a sunny afternoon and distribute Gospel tracts. Carey and I took the trumpet and the accordion so we could play hymns while the church people handed out the tracts. We were playing our 3rd or 4th hymn when four policemen marched up and arrested us. One of them announced that we were going to the police station. I started to take the accordion off, but he refused to let me do so. He said, "I want to have the evidence on you."

So, in the presence of hundreds of curious onlookers, we marched about five blocks through the center of Burgos with two policemen in front, Carey and I in the middle, and two policemen behind. When we arrived at Police Headquarters, I started to put the accordion down. Once again, the policeman said, "No, I want to have the evidence on you." We stood for an hour waiting for the Chief of Police to show up. (By the way—accordions are heavy!)

Perhaps a brief picture of the political status at that time will help to understand what happened next. General Franco had formed an alliance with the Catholic Church before winning the Spanish Civil War in 1938. In 1960 the political wheels were turning in all of Europe, and Spain wanted to form part of the European Union. However, it had two deterrents: the dictatorial form of government and the intolerance of all religious groups outside of the official state religion. Evidently, with the goal of entering the European Union, Spain had passed a religious liberty law in 1967, but the military dictatorship and the alliance were still strong in 1972.

Well, here we were at Police Headquarters with trumpet and accordion, having been arrested for playing hymns and distributing tracts. When the Chief finally arrived, he didn't quite know what to do with us. (Had it been 10 years earlier, before the passing of the Religious Liberty Law, we'd have been locked in jail long before the Chief ever showed up.) After consulting with the other officials, he said, "We're going to let you go this time. But if you want to keep doing what you're doing, you will have to go out into the country where there are no people." Imagine that!

One thing is for sure. If I ever have another open-air meeting in Burgos, I'll take my flute along, just in case.

TWENTY-FOUR
He's Got Fire in His Eyes

IGNACIO DEL Río is one of the most intriguing Spaniards I have ever met. He is a gifted artist. He has that uncanny ability to observe the minute, almost imperceptible nuances of personality. He seems to look right into the mind and character of an individual.

Our dear friends, Carl and Carole Blyth, along with Frank and Flora Jean Garlock came to Burgos to help us record our second LP sacred album. After the recording was complete, we took the four of them to the little village of Ubierna to visit Ignacio and his friend, Sussanne, originally from California. We had asked Ignacio to do an oil painting of Flora Jean out of appreciation for all her help on the piano.

Since Sussanne was an American, it didn't take long for the seven of us to get into a buzz of conversation. Ignacio was intently observing us. All of a sudden, he interrupted and said, "I want to paint Frank. He's got fire in his eyes."

Frank didn't speak Spanish in those days, so I translated what Ignacio had said about him. Frank responded, "Yes, I've got fire in my eyes, but it is under control now since

God saved me." (I might add that anyone who has heard Flora Jean play the piano knows that she has fire in her fingers!)

Ignacio did produce beautiful paintings of both Frank and Flora Jean. These masterful oil paintings presently grace the hallway at the entrance of Ron (Patch the Pirate) and Shelly Hamilton's home.

We continued to cultivate our friendship with Ignacio and Sussanne. We witnessed to them and explained the Gospel on several occasions. We suspected that their relationship was shaky. Ignacio drank a lot, and when he was drunk, he often had an uncontrollable temper. We kept telling them that God could save them and give them new life through Christ. Ignacio claimed not to believe in God. He often said, "For me, nature is everything."

I often wondered why Ignacio, with his superior powers of observation, could not see that even "*the heavens declare the glory of God.*" Why couldn't he understand Romans 1:20—that everything that he observed in nature around him revealed God's power? I could only think of II Corinthians 4, that the god of this world had blinded the gifted eyes of this artist so that he could not see the clearly revealed truth of the Gospel.

Then one day, the truth came out. At about 4:00 a.m. one Sunday morning, Ignacio came banging on our door, half drunk. We got dressed, and Margaret made a pot of coffee. Now, under the effects of alcohol and unable to control his emotions, he begged me not to speak about Jesus again. He said, "If I were to accept Christ, everything would have to change. I would lose my friends. My whole philosophy of art would have to change. Please don't talk to me anymore about Jesus."

Shortly after that, Sussanne took the children and moved to Southern Spain, somewhere near Portugal. Our team moved to Elche, and we heard later that Ignacio had moved to South America. We have not seen him since. We have prayed for him, and we trust that someone else was able to water the seed that had been sown.

We will never forget Ignacio. We have two treasured reminders of a unique individual and a gifted painter. His painting called "Castilla" hangs in the home of our daughter Debbie, and Margaret and I have a lovely Ignacio del Río painting of Becky and Mimi playing their flutes.

TWENTY-FIVE
A Cup of Coffee with the Governor

OUR MISSIONARY team moved to Spain in 1971, during the final years of a repressive dictatorship led by General Franco. After a survey trip and a time of prayer, we chose the city of Burgos to begin our first church. It was a very conservative city in the heart of old Castil. Burgos was best known for its impressive Gothic cathedral. Four miles outside of Burgos, Margaret and I found a quaint town called Quintanadueñas, with a population of 150 people. We rented one side of a rock house that was built in 1637. (Actually, it was a house/barn with the animals living downstairs. Our neighbor, who lived in the other half, had two oxen and some pigs on the ground floor.)

We soon discovered that the maximum authority in our town was the local Catholic priest. He was very much upset over our arrival. As best I can recall, he only talked with me once in the four years we lived there. That conversation was shortly after our arrival, and he informed me that all of the people in town were his sheep and if we convinced anyone to go with us, we would be guilty of sheep stealing. He also informed me that Spain was a Christian nation, and that if we wanted to be missionaries we should go to India or some other heathen nation.

One day my neighbor, who lived in the other half of the rock house, helped me install a heater. When we finished the job he said, "Today I have committed a mortal sin." Now that sounded really bad to me, so I asked him what he had done. He told me, "The priest said that anyone who entered your house would be guilty of committing a mortal sin. Today I entered your house."

The priest went to the mayor of our town and told him to get the heretics (us) out of town. The mayor had no idea what to do or how to go about it, so the priest told him to go to the governor of the province. We found out later that, even though the governor was Catholic and his wife a member of the powerful Opus Dei, he told the mayor they couldn't expel us just because we weren't Catholic. He reminded the mayor that Spain passed a religious liberty law in 1967, and we could legally live there.

But the priest was a persistent man. When a new school was inaugurated in our town, he invited five additional priests to the inauguration and asked the governor to be the special speaker. I heard about the planned inaugural speech, so I took my camera and stood in the back where I could hear. (Credit where credit is due—the governor was eloquent.) With a powerful voice, punctuated with frequent dramatic pauses, the distinguished Governor made an emotional speech filled with high and lofty meaningless political words. Then to conclude his oration, with a vocabulary that would make Cervantes jealous, he almost wept for the mother country as he declared that his beloved Spain would always be the land of the Blessed Virgin.

When he had completed his colorful dissertation, he walked out of the church with the local priest. I got some excellent close-up photos of the two. The priest pointed me out to the governor, and I could almost hear him declaring that I was the guilty, sheep-stealing heretic.

About two weeks later, I was distributing tracts and Gospels of John in downtown Burgos. It was a cold morning. In fact, it was almost always cold in Burgos. After a time of distribution, I stepped into Cafeteria Roma to have a cup of coffee. I sat down at a table and picked up a newspaper. Much to my surprise, I saw the governor walk in and up to the counter just a few feet from where I was seated. I heard him order a café con leche (coffee with milk). I quietly stepped up beside the governor and also asked for a café con leche. Then I opened the conversation by asking him if he were the governor.

As we started talking, he realized that I was a foreigner but complimented me on my Spanish. (I still had a Chilean accent.) I spared no words to express my deepest appreciation for the picturesque city of Burgos. Then he asked me, "How did you know I was the governor?" So I told him that I was the Protestant missionary living in Quintanadueñas and that I heard his inaugural speech two weeks earlier at the Catholic Church.

All of the sudden, his eloquence vanished, and in a stammering manner he asked, "W-well, h-how are things going?"

I told him, "Great! We just baptized two people last week."

At that moment, the waiter served us both our café con leche. The kind governor picked up his cup and drank his coffee without stopping. He immediately said, "Goodbye." And he left. I noticed that his face was red.

Then I tried my coffee. It was too hot to drink! It took me about five minutes to get it down. Now, I had no malice in my heart toward the distinguished governor. It was not my intention to inflict pain and suffering, but I am quite sure that he parched his eloquent tongue. He probably scorched his distinguished tonsils!

I had to go immediately and relate the incident to Margaret. I don't guess I felt very sorry for him. In fact, I confess, I laughed half of the way home!

TWENTY-SIX
Getting Buttered Up

IT IS quite an adventure to drive half way around the country of Mexico in a 25-foot motorhome. In the 1980s, I would say that the Mexican back roads were not made for motorhome travel.

But Frank and Ruth Buie are adventurous, and with Margaret and me as guides, we did it! We crossed several rivers where bridges had not yet been built, and we put the motorhome on three different ferries to cross other rivers.

We almost turned back at one point when we came to what appeared to be a shallow river, but it had an open stream of water over 200 feet wide! While we were trying to decide what to do, a local taxi driver came over to talk to us about the crossing. He got down and looked under the motor home. He then said, "I'll show you where to cross, and I think you can make it. But there are three big rocks just under the surface that you will have to avoid." No problem. Since Debbie, Becky, and Mimi loved to find an excuse for getting in the water, he pointed out the rocks, and our girls waded out and found them. So with a daughter standing on each rock, we proceeded. During the last 15 to 20 feet, the motor started sputtering.

Frank knew immediately what had happened. (In his younger years he had been an expert mechanic.) A few days before our river incident, we had crossed the 10,000-foot high Rio Frio mountain pass between Mexico City and Puebla. In order to get the proper air-gas mixture at that high altitude, Frank had taken the top off the air filter and turned it upside down. That little trick had solved our high altitude air intake problem, but now it almost sunk us in the river by letting water filter in. The motor sputtered, but we made it!

We eventually came to another stream that was obviously shallow, but the problem there was that the bank was too steep. Nevertheless, we cautiously drove down the steep incline. But when the front wheels reached the center of the little stream, the backend of our Winnebago got hung on the bank! So here we were, up a creek without a paddle (or shovel)! I saw one house nearby and was able to borrow a shovel. Frank and I started digging. News of our predicament got around fast. Within a few minutes, about a dozen men and boys showed up. They told us to get in and drive, and they would push. And did they ever push! They got us going, and in the process, they pushed so hard that the back of the motorhome was bent in a couple of inches for the remainder of our trip!

For one of the bigger rivers, we put the motorhome on a ferry. We met a lovely couple on that ferry. It was getting late in the afternoon, so the man told us, "We are going to my Dad's hacienda. Just follow me when we get off, and you can camp out on our farm tonight." It was indeed a picturesque old hacienda with plenty of horses, cattle, and a few donkeys running around.

We ate our supper and went to bed. At about 2:00 a.m., someone came banging on the door and woke us all up. When I opened the door, I was bombarded with the stench of alcohol. Our untimely visitor was drunk! He said he was hungry and wanted something to eat. I was not very happy with this visitor, but I gave him a hamburger bun. That didn't satisfy him. He opened the bun and said he wanted some meat on it. Now my mood was not improving. I pretended to not know what he was asking for. Even in his drunken condition, he was resourceful. He put the bun down and put his fists to his head with his index fingers extended and started saying Mooo, Moo.

I could hardly keep from laughing, but I just put my hands out in a helpless gesture and said, "I'm sorry." With that, he left, and we went back to sleep.

About a half hour later, he came back and knocked again. When I opened the door, he had a big smile on his face and handed me a fresh homemade cake of butter. It had been churned right there on the farm. Well, that did it. Drunk or not, he knew how to "butter us up." I can't remember just what we had in our little refrigerator, but we always kept lettuce, tomatoes, cheese, etc. Anyway, we made him a thick sandwich with lots of butter on it. Now he was happy. And he was talkative. I think he would have talked all night.

Finally, I told him we were all very sleepy. We thanked him for the butter and told him "good night" and closed the door. We all had a good laugh about our sleep interruption and went back to bed, just a motorhome full of happy campers!

TWENTY-SEVEN
Attacked by a Lion

SINCE MY college days, I have had a big interest in Mexico. I will admit that I have not read much about Mexican wildlife. From my first visits to Mexico, I saw snakes, iguanas, and scorpions. I had heard that there were foxes, wolves, and wild boar in the mountains, and maybe wildcats. In my wildest imagination I never expected to see with my own eyes, an African lion in Mexico, much less be attacked by one! But I am alive today to tell you that it really did happen.

The attack was on our second motorhome tour of Mexico with Frank and Ruth Buie. Faith Christian Missions was interested in helping my good friend and college roommate, Jose Lara, with his Bible Institute and church planting ministry in the mountains of the state of Hidalgo. The trip also afforded us the opportunity to revisit the Latin American hospital in Puebla where our three lovely daughters were born.

One morning as we were on a leisurely drive toward southern Mexico, we saw a huge sign advertising a jungle safari. Even though I had traveled through many parts of Mexico with our evangelistic team, I couldn't remember ever seeing a safari sign. This one merited investigation.

We were not disappointed. We entered the compound, paid for the drive-through tour, and started slowly moving through the indicated route. The first excitement came when a huge leopard walked out in front of our motorhome and put his menacing paws on the front windshield. I found myself about 30 inches from an enormous pair of green eyes that were staring into my pale white face.

Fortunately, the safari guards, carrying a stun gun, saw the leopard approach our motorhome and immediately drove up with horn blowing and scared the animal away. We assumed it was the smell of food in the vehicle that attracted the animal. But even that was not a pleasant thought since we carried mostly vegetables on our trips, and leopards are carnivorous.

However, that wasn't the end of our excitement. Just a few hundred feet on down the trail, a more cunning animal attacked. And just like the devil would do, this huge roaring lion attacked us from behind where the guards could not see him! The enormous animal reared up on his hind feet and began pawing and biting our spare tire. We rushed to the back of the motorhome and saw him start ripping off the spare tire cover. In an exceptionally alarmed voice, Margaret yelled at me, "Honey, don't let him take our tire cover!"

Well, I admit that I sometimes go to great lengths to support the exaggerated concept that Margaret has of my bravery, but a lion is the limit! I just told her, "Honey, we'll let him keep the cover, and he can have the spare tire too if he wants it. I'm not getting out of this motorhome!"

The incident reminded me of a country gospel song that my three elder siblings, (Mildred, Bronner, and Violet) used to sing when I was a child. The song was about Noah's ark. The words to the first lines of the chorus were, "I had rather be on the inside looking out, than to be on the outside looking in."

The Buies still have a picture of that shameless thieving lion walking away with our stolen tire cover in its mouth. It is even turned in the right direction to be able to easily read the "W" for Winnebago.

TWENTY-EIGHT
A Church Split

A DIVISION is not a new occurrence. It happens everywhere. It happens in the USA. It happens in Spain. It happened in our church in Elche, no less—the Emmanuel Baptist Church (La Iglesia Bautista Emanuel)! Not only that, it happened when the church was growing, and there was a spirit of excitement. We were having 80 to 100 people attend every Sunday. Souls were being saved regularly, and we were baptizing new converts in the Mediterranean Sea in early May and late September. (We avoided going in the summer due to the shameful attire—or lack of it.)

But let me go back to the beginning. When Dennis Flower, Paul Bixby, and I brought our families to Elche to plant a new church, we didn't know anyone. Our first project was to cover the city with Gospel tracts; then we started Bible studies in our home. We bought folding chairs to accommodate the visitors. When we had grown to about 30 to 35 people, our team decided it was time to rent a building. We were able to rent a storefront with enough space to accommodate 70 to 75 people, and in April, 1977, we had the official organization of Emmanuel Baptist Church. Pretty soon, the 75 chairs were filling up. We were experiencing close fellowship! But we had a problem. We needed Sunday school classrooms.

Our landlady owned a second storefront which joined ours. Since we always paid our rent on time and kept the building in good repair, she was happy to have us rent the second one. That gave us a bigger auditorium and choir platform, but we still needed Sunday school rooms.

We saw the division coming, but of all people, it was a church planting, independent Baptist missionary that divided our church. As a matter of fact, it was Al Bonikowsky, father of my son-in-law, Andy Bonikowsky.

In part, it was because Pastor Al hasn't always been a missionary. He was a builder before God called him to the mission field. With his construction background, our deacons felt that he would be the best (and least expensive) man to come and divide our church and give us more Sunday school classes. He succeeded. By installing a series of folding doors, he split the church into sections and gave us the much-needed space. In fact, Al didn't even charge us for splitting the church. We paid for the materials, and he donated his work.

Actually, it was the second time we had called on Al for his expertise. Our first meeting place in Burgos was located in the small town of Quintanadueñas, and it looked something like a barn. We affectionately called it the Quintanaduenas Cathedral. Al consented to come and lay out the plans and help us build a bathroom.

More recently the Lord led our son-in-law, Andy, to purchase a 300-year-old Basque farmhouse/barn and convert it into a Bible Conference/Retreat Center. The quaint farmhouse was three stories high on one end and had rock walls that were nearly three feet thick. The crooked tree pole ceiling rafters and out-of-square doors and windows make the structure look like an architect's nightmare. I salute Al for being willing, in the sunset of his missionary service, to accept the monumental challenge of transforming the time-worn, dilapidated farmhouse into a beautiful, efficient, and comfortable building for a dynamic conference and retreat center. Under Al's supervision, and with the help of more than a dozen skilled work teams who have dedicated their time and talents for this missionary project, a magnificent transformation is underway.

During the 52 years Margaret and I have been privileged to serve the Lord on the mission field, we have observed gifted missionaries with tremendous talents and abilities which they have used for the Lord's honor and glory. (Fortunately, I believe Al is the only church splitting specialist we have known.)

What God-given talents do you have?

TWENTY-NINE
Four Walls and a Roof

A FEW years after planting Emmanuel Baptist Church in Elche, our team started praying about starting a Christian day school. Three or four families in our church really encouraged us to do so.

Tito and Milly Noel showed a special interest in the school. They had recently moved to Spain from Australia. They were living and working in a town about an hour's drive south of Elche. Tito told us that if we would start the Christian school where their children would be able to study, he would move his family to Elche and would commute for his work. He asked us to pray about housing for his family. He told us that he was a builder and all that he would need in Elche would be four walls and a roof.

We started praying, and very soon one of the ladies in our church found just what Tito was looking for. A young couple, who was engaged to be married, purchased a huge lot in a new subdivision a few miles outside of town and started building their house. By the time they got the outside walls built and the roof on, the lady decided she didn't want to live in "the country." They abandoned the project, and Tito purchased their "four walls and a roof" just for the price of the land!

The Christian school project went forward. With our limited facilities and personnel, we chose to start an ACE school (Accelerated Christian Education). The Lord gave us some good years in the school. Tito and Milly moved into their "four walls and a roof," and little by little their rustic dwelling place started looking like a home. Milly went through the ACE training program and became a valuable member of the school staff.

One unexpected blessing came because of the huge lot Tito had bought. Some church people provided volunteer work for their home project, but more importantly, it became the sports center for our young people and a picnic area for the entire church. Eventually, Tito converted their four walls and a roof into a beautiful Swiss-style chalet.

I must say that our team discovered that it takes a lot of time and effort to run a Christian school. Our wives helped. Milly Noel helped. But Dennis Flower, Paul Bixby and I began to realize that the school was taking a lot of time away from the church ministry in Elche and Alicante. With enrollment growing, we prayed that the Lord would provide someone to help in the school. God laid it on the hearts of Mike and Madelaine Dodgens to come as teachers. Things went well for a few years, and the school had a big impact on the lives of some of our church families.

Unfortunately, there came a time when construction came to a standstill. Tito and Milly were a key family in our school and church, but the construction bubble left Tito unemployed. After much prayer and many tears, Tito and Milly moved back to Australia.

About that same time, the school started facing a bit of opposition. The provincial Director of Education complained that our installations did not meet all the requirements for sports, safety, etc. He said that our school was illegal and threatened to denounce us to the Department of Education. We finally had to face the fact that our primary purpose for being in Spain was for church planting, and we should not run the risk of getting kicked out of the country for failure to meet all the school standards.

After 10 years, we closed the school. Mike and Madelaine, however, had more than earned their place in our team, and they stayed with us and helped in many facets of the ministry until 2008 when they moved north to form part of the Aierdi team with my son-in-law, Andy Bonikowsky.

Permit me to add an amazing anecdote to the school story. Twenty-five years ago, a bucket of tears was shed when Tito and Milly had to say goodbye to all their dear friends at the Christian school and church for their return to Australia. However, as I write this story, they are again our neighbors in Greenville, SC. I would love to share with you all the fascinating details that brought about this delightful change, but that would have to be another story!

THIRTY
Will You At Least Pray About It?

WHEN THE phone rang late on Saturday night, I couldn't help but be a little bit apprehensive. Margaret and I had received many of those calls over the years—sickness, car trouble, the maternity ward, last minute schedule changes, etc.

In the middle of January, 1998, the Saturday night call came from my friend, Dr. Frank Garlock—a patient, but demanding, music professor. I was not prepared for this one. Dr. Garlock told me that his good friend, Dr. Carl Herbster, was helping start a Christian university in Monterrey, Mexico, and they were calling to invite me to move to Mexico and head up the music department. The school would be called The Christian University of the Americas (La Universidad Cristiana de Las Americas, UCLA, no less). My apprehension then turned to shock.

My first reaction was that the job was too big for me, and even if it weren't, the timing was wrong. Margaret and I were busy and happy, working in a missionary team on the other side of the pond. We were very much involved in the Emmanuel Baptist Church and Bible Institute. We were also helping in a mission church. I tried to politely tell Dr. Garlock and Dr. Herbster that it would not be possible, but I thanked them for their confidence.

I discovered that Dr. Herbster does not accept a "no" answer very easily. He came up with some imaginative reasons to try to convince me. Of course, I realized that a time of transition would eventually come in the Spain ministry but also knew that we were not ready for it then. We were also not ready for a move to a different country. We didn't have a man trained to take over the ministry. We would definitely need to pray a lot and seek counsel before making such a life-changing decision. It was not a short conversation. Finally, Dr. Herbster asked, "Would you at least pray about it?" And I reluctantly said, "Yes, I will pray about it, but we can't go."

Well, Margaret and I did pray, and we sought Godly counsel. I discussed it with the pastor of our sending church. My coworker, Dennis Flower, and I discussed it at length. If I were to leave, it would put a lot more responsibility on him. We continued to receive more phone calls from Dr. Herbster giving additional reasons why it had to be us. Finally, with the approval of our team and our pastor, we agreed to take a one-year leave of absence (which we later extended for an additional year) and move to Monterrey during the summer of 1998.

Looking back on that difficult decision, we can now say that it was a wonderful decision, which led us into two of the most fruitful years of our 52 years on the mission field. Time and space will not permit me to relate the manifold blessings and challenges that we encountered in Monterrey. I will only mention two for the moment.

First of all, the privilege of working with Pastor Julio Montes, pastor of Gennesaret Baptist Church and director of the Christian University, was one of the highlights of our missionary service. He was one of the most Godly, consistent, humble, and may I say, most competent Christian men I have ever known. I thank God for his vision and dedication. I will not say more at this time because I would like to dedicate a separate chapter to his memory and to the outreach of the Christian University of the Americas.

The second blessing came through one of our first-year university students, Alberto Zermeño. I soon discovered that Alberto was brilliant, dedicated, and consistent. I had him in all of my classes for two years and considered him one of my very best students.

Margaret and I returned to Spain after two fantastic years in Monterrey. As we saw the time approaching for a transition from missionary to national pastor in Spain, we spent a lot of time in prayer. Meanwhile, Alberto had graduated from UCLA, earned a Masters degree at Bob Jones University, and had married a lovely Spanish lady, Laura, from Barcelona. The more Dennis Flower and I prayed and searched for a future pastor, the more we became convinced that Alberto was the ideal candidate for the position.

In 2013, Emmanuel Baptist Church in Elche, Spain, voted to call Alberto Zermeño to take the reins of the ministry. As I write this, I can say that Pastor Alberto and Laura are doing a wonderful job.

I thank the Lord for letting me serve Him in Monterrey for two years. Thank you, Dr. Garlock, for your recommendation and encouragement. And thank you, Dr. Herbster, for your confidence and your persistent phone calls.

Thirty-One
I Will Get Out of Prison Someday

WHEN A convicted murderer was sentenced to prison by a highly respected federal judge named Julio Montes, his threatening response was, "I will get out of prison someday, but when I do, you won't get out of the grave.

It was my privilege to meet Pastor Julio Montes in the summer of 1998, just prior to the opening of the Christian University of the Americas (UCLA) in Monterrey, Mexico. He had renounced his distinguished position as Federal Judge in order to become the director of the new university. He was also pastor of Gennesaret Baptist Church. Margaret and I had taken a leave of absence from Spain so that I could organize a Music Department for the new university. For the next two years, it was my privilege to serve under this Godly, dedicated, and extremely efficient man.

Julio Montes was born in 1950 in a small town in the province of Nuevo Leon, Mexico. He was the second of nine brothers and sisters, and as a young boy, became the shepherd of his father's sheep. Julio's father was unsaved; nevertheless, Julio heard the Gospel from his mother and grandfather. At the tender age of nine, he gave his heart and life to God.

Julio was an exceptionally bright student. After having graduated from high school at age 15, he moved to Monterrey to enter a Baptist seminary and prepare himself for the pastorate. The director of the seminary told Julio that the Mexican churches were poor and would not be able to pay him a livable salary and insisted that he also enter the university and study for a career. His first career choice would have been medicine; but since he had no money for books, he reluctantly chose law, knowing that he could do all of his studying in the library. That providential choice opened doors at every turn in his future ministry.

Julio worked as cook in order to pay for his studies while in seminary. For his extension ministry, he was assigned to a new mission work in the town of Guadalupe. Another student by the name of Rosario Ibarra was also chosen to help in the new mission work. In 1976, Julio and Rosario were united in marriage to form a husband-wife team for the rest of their lives.

That same year, the mission was organized into Gennesaret Baptist Church, with Julio Montes as pastor. One year later, in 1977, Pastor Julio graduated from law school. Almost immediately, he secured a law position working for the federal government of Monterrey. While still in his 20s, he was promoted to the very respectable position of Federal Judge.

Even though his time was divided between his demands as judge and his ever-growing responsibilities as husband and also pastor of Gennesaret Baptist Church, God blessed his ministry in a very special way.

For several years, Pastor Montes served as family judge. In that position he was able to counsel many couples who came to him seeking divorce and left his office as newborn Christians, with a new commitment to save their marriage.

Pastor Julio told me that on one occasion Nora, a distraught female government lawyer, came to him for counsel. She was unsaved and had recently gotten a divorce from her husband, Sergio, who was also a government lawyer. Pastor Julio and Rosario befriended Nora and started witnessing to her about Christ. They started taking her to church with them every Sunday. Within a few weeks, they led Nora to Christ. Then the three of them started praying for Sergio. Nine months later, he got saved. Pastor Julio re-married them. He told me, "That's the only divorced couple I have ever married."

Sergio and Nora's lives were transformed by the grace of God. Presently, they are active members of Gennesaret Baptist Church. During the two years that I was serving at UCLA, this converted government lawyer took me bowling three times. I guess all stories have an unhappy element, and this one is no exception. Sergio beat me every single game we played!

In 1991, Dr. Carl Herbster invited Pastor Montes to a missions conference in Kansas City, Missouri. His church also operated a Christian school. Having served in the judicial system for many years, Pastor Montes had seen the increasing number of rebellious teenagers who were ruining their lives through drugs and alcohol. As he saw the contrast with the well-behaved and respectable children and young people in the Christian school, God laid the burden on his heart to start a Christian school in Monterrey. The Lord led him to the right people in authority who were willing to help a pastor and judge start a school. In 1992, Pastor Montes started Mexico's first official Christian school. The school grew from kindergarten through junior high, but Pastor Julio was still not satisfied. He became more and more burdened to expand to the high school and university level.

This dream became a reality in 1998 with a small high school and 19 university students. Now, 17 years later, there are close to 200 university students with dozens of graduates serving as pastors, teachers, and various other occupations. UCLA presently has graduates serving as missionaries in eight foreign countries.

Under Pastor Julio's leadership, God has continued to bless Gennesaret Baptist Church. With over 600 people attending each Sunday, it has become necessary to have double services. But apart from that, a half dozen Independent Baptist churches have been started out of the mother church, with another five or six mission churches at different stages of development at the present time.

In the early years of his government job, Pastor served three years as Criminal Judge. During that time he presided over a murder case where the evidence was overwhelming. He had no choice but to sentence the guilty man to prison. When Judge Montes declared the prison sentence, the enraged man shouted, "I will get out of prison someday, but when I do, you won't get out of the grave!"

Several years later, a man came to Pastor Julio after one of the church services and told him, "My brother is in prison, and he really needs to talk with a pastor. Would you go visit him?"

Pastor Julio agreed to make the visit. When he located the man's cell, the prisoner said, "I know you. You are the man who sent me here."

Judge Montes had ordered this criminal to be placed behind bars. But that afternoon, in the name of the Judge of all the earth, Pastor Julio was able to give him the Gospel message of forgiveness and salvation through faith in Christ and see his soul set free. The chains of sin that had bound him for so many years were broken that afternoon as he, by faith, became a new creation in Christ.

Sad to say, I received a late Saturday night call on October 4, 2014, informing me that Pastor Julio Montes and his beloved wife, Rosario, had died in a tragic automobile accident. I was shocked. It was difficult to believe even though I know that God makes no mistakes. I cannot imagine how much the members of Gennesaret Baptist Church and the personnel and students of the Christian University of the Americas are grieving. They have suffered a great loss. I personally feel that I have lost one of the most respected and Godly friends that I have been privileged to work under.

Dr. Frank Garlock, Margaret, and I went to Monterrey to participate in the memorial service for Dr. and Mrs. Montes at Gennesaret Baptist church on October 10. The three Montes daughters were sitting on the front row of the church, and they encouraged us by their unwavering trust in the goodness of the Lord in a very difficult situation.

It was especially difficult for Perla, the oldest daughter, since she was driving the car when a tire blew and the car went out of control, killing both of her parents. She too was injured but was allowed to leave the hospital and come to the church service and be a blessing to the large group of mourners who were there.

We were also encouraged by the unquestioning response of the church and its leadership as well as the leadership of the university. We are trusting the Lord to lead them to the right man, or men that God in His wisdom has chosen to continue the work that was started by Julio Montes. The work is not only having a great influence in Mexico but in several other Spanish-speaking countries as well.

Pastor Julio's life and ministry had a great impact on me. My life and Margaret's were greatly enriched as a result of serving with Pastor Julio and his wife Rosario. They will be greatly missed but never forgotten.

Thirty-Two
Midnight and No Place to Sleep

M ARGARET AND I have had the privilege of traveling to several different countries with Frank and
Ruth Buie. Frank has a heart for missions and has visited
and helped missionaries in many parts of the world.

On a trip with the Buies to Portugal, we encountered a
slight difficulty. We had conducted meetings with some
missionaries in Rota, Spain, and had decided to take the
long route home, by way of Portugal. Leaving Spain, we
put the car on a ferry and entered Portugal at the border
town of Ayamonte. We were counting this trip as a mini
vacation, and I admit we had not done an excessive amount
of preparation. Our plan was to see the lovely vacation
area of Faro, with its famous beaches, and then continue
on to Lisbon.

Actually, Portugal is a very small country, but we had not
counted on inclement weather. First of all, we got caught
in a powerful rain storm, but we kept driving. We later
hit dense fog in the mountains, but we kept driving. We
continued driving because we could not find a place to
stop! I believe all four of us were still quite adventurous in
the 1980s, but none of us wanted to drive all night, nor
sleep in the car on some foggy mountain curve.

Finally we came to a village with perhaps four or five houses. The town did not have a hotel or a motel. It did not have a Youth Hostel, and as far as we knew, up until that time, it did not have a Bed and Breakfast. We did find a house with the lights on and decided to investigate. Frankly, our situation was not too good. To make matters worse, none of us spoke Portuguese. We knocked, and a kind elderly lady came to the door. She didn't speak English or Spanish. In the next few minutes we invented all kinds of sign language as we spoke many unintelligible words. We were becoming a bit apprehensive. Remember, this occurred back in the '80s and, frankly, none of us were spring chickens! We were tired and looking for a place to sleep.

Obviously this elderly lady had high moral standards. She kept trying to communicate with us through sign language and the most elementary form of vocabulary. We could tell by the inflection of her voice that she was asking questions. When she asked "Mama? Papa?," we finally realized that she wanted to make sure we were married couples. We nodded yes, hugged our wives, and showed her our wedding rings.

She found us two rooms.

I'm so glad the Lord gave me Margaret. And just for the record, we have been legally and happily married since 1959.

THIRTY-THREE
Not Scared –
Just a Bit Apprehensive

THE YEAR 1980 brought about a big adjustment for Margaret and me. We took a year of furlough to visit our supporting churches and to be in Greenville, South Carolina, for Debbie to enter Bob Jones University while Becky and Mimi completed their last year of high school.

When furlough ended, Margaret and I shed an impressive number of tears when we said goodbye to our *three* university students and boarded a plane for Spain. For the first time in nineteen years, our nest was empty. On more than one occasion during the following months, we set the table for *five* out of sheer habit.

The nest didn't stay empty for long, however. A missionary in Madrid contacted us and made plans to visit us and bring his 20-year-old cousin to meet us. Her name was Joy McAuley, and she, like our three, was a university student. Joy was a Spanish major in Queen's University of Belfast, Northern Ireland. The University had sent her to Spain to teach English in a school in our province of Alicante for a year while she studied Spanish.

When we were introduced, I got the impression that Joy was timid. To make casual conversation I said, "Joy, this is a big step for a young girl to come to a foreign country with a different language and culture. Are you scared?"

She answered, "No, not scared—just a bit apprehensive."

We soon realized that she was not timid but was, in fact, a dedicated Christian with strong convictions. She was not timid about sharing her faith. She grew up in a Free Presbyterian church where Rev. Ian Paisley was the moderator. (Six months later, she asked me for Biblical baptism. It was my privilege to baptize her in the Mediterranean Sea!)

The initial plan was for Joy to come to Elche by train on Sundays, attend the morning church service, have lunch with us, and return to her town of Villajoyosa in the afternoon. She won our hearts immediately. After one more visit, Joy commented, "If it would be possible for me to spend the night here on Sunday night, I could go to choir practice and the evening service." We had three empty beds, so we gladly accepted her brilliant idea.

The following week, she had another brilliant idea. "If I were to come on Saturday afternoon, I could attend young people's meeting!" Idea accepted.

Two weeks later, Joy bounced in with her effervescent personality and winning Colgate smile and announced, "I have been able to arrange my schedule so that I can now come on Friday afternoon and stay until Monday morning!" Another favorable, brilliant idea.

Oh yes, I should have mentioned that, beginning with her first visit, she always brought Margaret and me a delicious box of chocolate covered almonds, a sweet gesture that helped win our hearts.

Now, let me digress a few years. The first young person that I baptized in Elche, in the Mediterranean Sea, was Moisés Pérez. I taught him guitar. He is still one of the favorite tenor soloists in Emmanuel Baptist Church. As a teenager, Moisés volunteered as a Red Cross worker. He invited his buddies to church. One of them, José Bernabeu, lived only a block and a half from our house. José and Moisés became good friends with our three daughters. Many evenings we would have six or eight young visitors.

Our three daughters and Moisés talked with José about his need for salvation, and on one very special day, Debbie led him to Christ. From that very first day when José got saved, he never looked back. He continued his studies in electronics and also entered our night Bible Institute.

Now we will fast forward to the Joy chapters. Moisés and José had become leaders in our youth group. Moisés had his eyes on a cute little Andalusian girl named Mayte that he had met at Mount Calvary Baptist camp. But José had eyes only for Joy. Now it was my time to become a bit apprehensive. Joy was practically our "adopted daughter" by this time. I told her that while she was in our home, she would be under our house rules. If a boy wanted to invite her out, he had to first get my permission. Joy (and her parents) was happy with the arrangement. Needless to say, José and I got well acquainted during the next few months. Time will not permit me to tell of José and Joy's storybook romance that followed.

Dennis Flower, Paul Bixby, and I realized that José was progressing well in our Bible Institute. It was obvious from his early days in the Institute that he had a pastor's heart. When our Elche church started a mission in Alicante (capital of our province), we asked José to help. Dennis, Paul, and I took turns helping in the mission church. David Bell also helped in Alicante for several years until he moved to Petrer to start a new church.

José faithfully carried out his extension ministry in Alicante week after week. He sold his apartment in Elche and moved to Alicante in order to dedicate more time to the ministry. José became the first "preacher boy" from our church to graduate from the Bible Institute. We later had the joy of ordaining him into the Gospel ministry.

Joy's studies of Spanish paid off. Over time, she became an excellent translator. She translated several hymns from English into Spanish that are included in *Himnos Majestuosos*. Joy also wrote the words in English for three of the hymns that I composed for my missionary cantata, *Here Am I, Lord*.

Now let me give you the end of this "short story" from my perspective. José and Joy each finished their studies and then got married. They have raised two model children. The mission church that José helped develop from the beginning has been organized into The Good News Baptist Church. José is now the pastor of this growing church, and our Joy is by his side, encouraging him all the way.

During our last few years in Spain, José and I met almost every Friday morning for coffee and to pray and discuss ministry matters. We went through some difficult times together. But José often quoted Acts 20:24, *"None of these things move me, neither count I my life dear unto myself, so that I might finish my course with joy."*

I greatly miss those times of fellowship. But it is a great joy to know that José now has his group of faithful young men and is committing to them the things which he has learned so that they *"shall be able to teach others also."* (II Timothy 2:2)

Additional Blessings

THIRTY-FOUR
Keeping Up with the Joneses

ONE OF the greatest side benefits or, better stated, extra blessings for a missionary is the privilege of rubbing shoulders with so many of God's choice servants. I have had the opportunity over the years of fellowshipping with Godly pastors, evangelists, conference speakers, educators, and musicians in many parts of the world. I have been greatly blessed and challenged through contact with these heroes of the faith.

Of course, there is no way that I could ever compile a list of these great servants. Yet I would be remiss if I did not at least give honor to some of them. In view of the fact that I received most of my training for the mission field at Bob Jones University, it seems logical that I begin with the Joneses.

Dr. Bob Jones, Sr., in his extensive evangelistic campaigns, realized that many young people were losing their faith as they entered secular colleges. Sensing God's leading in his life, he founded what is now known as Bob Jones University. However, since his heartbeat was in evangelism, he continued that ministry as long as he lived. In 1959, he spent almost five hours relating his evangelism experiences to our newly-formed Mexican Evangelistic Team. Then in 1960 we scheduled Dr. Jones for meetings in Mexico.

We arranged for a one-night meeting in the famous Balderas Bull Ring in Cuidad Juarez. René Zapata interpreted for Dr. Bob in that meeting, and I had the privilege of playing the piano. There were about 3,000 in attendance that night, and 150 people came forward at the invitation to accept Christ as Savior.

During the sermon, someone threw a rock over the side of the bull ring. It hit a young lady in the head causing an injury that required several stitches. The next morning Dr. Bob asked me if anyone knew who the injured lady was. He went on to say that he didn't want to leave town without sending her a bouquet of flowers!

We went on to Mexico City for meetings; then to Puebla. While we were in Puebla, Dr. Bob gave Margaret a $10 bill. He told her, "This is for you. Don't let Flay spend it."

Dr. Bob Jones, Sr., was a great servant of God and one of my heroes. He had a great burden for seeing lost souls come to Jesus. I am still thrilled when I read about the great citywide campaigns he conducted all across America winning multiplied thousands of souls to Christ.

In many ways, Dr. Bob Jones, Jr., was vastly different from his father. I had occasional contact with him while I was a student but later had the privilege of forming a warm friendship with him as I served as his interpreter on many occasions. He was a powerful and eloquent preacher.

In Santiago, Chile, I interpreted for him when he preached a sermon on Jesus Stilling the Waves. He stated that when, "with His voice of divine authority, He scolded the raging waves, they cowered back like a little puppy dog who tucks his tail between his legs at his master's scolding."

While we were having lunch that day, he said "you didn't translate the puppy dog just like I said it." (He understood a lot of Spanish.) I had to agree with him but told him that I thought I got the idea across. Then he said, "I just did it to test you!"

Dr. Bob, Jr., was an internationally known authority on Renaissance art. He loved to visit El Prado, Spain's famous art museum. However, on a trip through Spain, he accepted a last-minute invitation to come on down to Elche and preach for us rather than spending time at El Prado, as originally planned. Instead he spent time in our home and in our church for special meetings. He told me, "I feel like I'm sinning if I'm not preaching." I was enriched and encouraged as a result of my contact with Dr. Bob, Jr.

Dr. Bob, III, is younger than me. My brother, Gettys, had classes with him at Bob Jones Academy. Again, my acquaintance with him came primarily by interpreting for him. In a couple of the conferences where we didn't need an interpreter, I had the privilege of leading the singing. Dr. Bob, III, is sensitive to the needs of a congregation. He preached some powerful and uplifting sermons for us in Elche at a time when our church was going through some difficulties.

Margaret and I enjoyed a little getaway with Dr. Bob, III, and his wife, Beneth, when we took them to Granada to spend the night. The next day we visited the Alhambra, the famous Moorish Castle which was abandoned in 1492 when the re-conquistadors finally drove the last of the Moors out of Spain. With all the energy that Dr. Bob, III, has, it is hard to find time to relax when he is around; but our brief getaway was a time of fun as well as rest and relaxation. He has been a great example of a dedicated servant, and I always feel edified when we spend time together.

I have been with Dr. Stephen Jones in only two conferences: Tubingen, Germany in 1996 and Mar del Plata, Argentina, in 2006. I was blessed by his preaching and impressed with his humility and warm friendship.

I have been challenged, enriched, and edified by trying to keep up with the Joneses during the past six decades. I thank the Lord for the many opportunities that God has given me, just a plodding missionary, to rub shoulders with them and also with scores of other of His choicest servants.

Thirty-Five
We Need an Up-to-Date Hymnbook

WHEN THE Lord opened the door for Margaret and me to go to Monterrey, Mexico, to set up the Music Department for the new Christian University of the Americas, I found myself almost fulltime in a music ministry. I did teach the freshman Bible class; but apart from that, most of my time was spent in teaching music theory, choir rehearsals, orchestra rehearsals, private music lessons, and writing arrangements for special music.

In the Gennesaret Baptist Church I usually led the congregational singing or played the piano for the services. I was practically immersed in musical activities 24/7. The popular Spanish hymnbook that we had used for many years in Spain was now out of print. I found myself spending hours searching for good, fresh, up-to-date hymns and arrangements in Spanish.

About that time, Mr. Frank Buie, founder of Faith Christian Missions, and his wife, Ruth, came to Monterrey to visit us. One day, in a casual conversation with Mr. Buie, I said, "We need an up-to-date Spanish hymnbook."

Without a moment's hesitation, Mr. Buie said, "If we need one, let's print one."

At the time, I had no idea how deeply his response would impact the next few years of our ministry.

In fact, his statement would have a much bigger impact on the lives of my longtime coworkers, Dennis and Ruth Ann Flower. In our team, we called Dennis Flower our theologian because of his consistent in-depth study of the Word. But Dennis is also a gifted and well-trained musician, and he has mastered the use of the Finale musical notation program. Not only that, his wife, Ruth Ann, is a gifted writer and translator of poetry.

We struck gold when we talked with Dr. Frank Garlock at Majesty Music about the idea. He had recently published his outstanding hymnbook, Majesty Hymns. Dr. Garlock gave us permission to use the Majesty Hymnbook format substituting Spanish words for the English ones.

Mr. Buie realized the potential of this project and immediately approved work scholarships for Alberto Zermeño, a freshman at the new Christian University, and for his sister, Denisse, to start typesetting the Spanish words. Dennis Flower started the notation for favorite Spanish hymns not found in the English hymnbook. Ruth Ann Flower started translating favorite new English hymns which had never before been translated into Spanish. Faith Christian Missions put up the funds for the preparation work as well as the printing of the final project.

Obviously, none of us could work fulltime on the hymn-book project because of all our other responsibilities in our church and Bible Institute. However, five years later, due largely to the persistence and perspiration of Dennis and Ruth Ann Flower, prodded along by Dr. Garlock, we printed the first edition of "*Himnos Majestuosos.*"

As of this writing, we are in our fourth printing with some 30,000 hymnbooks in circulation. Churches all over Spain, Central, and South America are now singing the more than 600 hymns included in this up-to-date hymnbook. Hundreds of Hispanic Churches springing up all over the USA are using it in their worship of our wonderful Lord. We have received dozens of emails and letters from all over the Spanish-speaking world telling us of the blessing the hymnbook has been to them.*

We have no way of knowing how it will be used in the future if the Lord delays His return. Mr. Buie told me one time that his desire was to accomplish something for the Lord during his lifetime that would continue to be used after he is gone. I believe he had that in mind when he founded Faith Christian Missions. I trust that his desire will also be accomplished through the publication of *Himnos Majestuosos.*

*See Appendix for further information about ordering

And may I ask, what are you doing that will have an influence on the spread of the Gospel after you are gone?

Thirty-Six
Climbing Up into the Van

IN OUR missionary travels, God has given us a multitude of close friends scattered throughout the USA and beyond. There is no way to name them all, but in this story, I will mention four.

My two college buddies, who form part of our "friends to the end" trio, are Pastor Larry Hufhand and businessman Terry Doane. They both live in Indiana. They have visited us in Spain. Pastor Larry has supported our family through the years and has recommended us to his pastor friends, some of whom have also supported us. Terry has encouraged us, prayed for us, and supported us financially. Some of my best clothing comes as a result of Terry's wife permitting me to raid his clothes closet. The Doanes also made it possible for Margaret and me to take a trip to the Holy Land.

But coming closer to home, let me mention Bob and Betty Miller. We also met during our college days and have remained friends for about 60 years. In preparation for some sacred music recordings, we sent Fran Barrero, our young "engineer," to Greenville for some recording studio training. Bob and Betty gave him room, board, and transportation. When Fran got married a few years ago, Bob and Betty came to Spain to celebrate his wedding with us.

On earlier furloughs, Bob and I would take his two dirt bikes out and hit the backwoods trails, and sometimes, even mountain trails. The years have gone by very quickly. Now for enjoyment, Bob and I are down to a calm game of ping pong now and then. (I usually let Bob beat me so he won't become discouraged.)

Margaret and I left Spain near the end of 2013, and I am now the director of Faith Christian Missions (FCMI). The mission provided a van for us to use. Since Margaret is small, I bought a stool to keep in the van to make it easier for her to climb in. (She weighed 98 pounds when we got married. Now, 55 years later, she has gained up to 100.)

We had been home only a couple of days when Bob and Betty drove by and saw Margaret climbing up into the van. They just blew the horn, waved, and drove on by.

A few days later, after spending time at BJU Missions Emphasis Week interviewing prospective missionary candidates or short term workers and encouraging all the students to pray for missionaries, Margaret and I came home quite tired. We had a bite to eat, and then Margaret went to bed. I stayed up to do some correspondence.

At about 10:00 p.m., Bob and Betty came banging on the side door and said they wanted to come in and talk with us. It was obvious that they were up to something special. I didn't know what was up, but with all the excitement, I could practically feel the static in the air. So I woke Margaret and told her to get dressed.

When Margaret came in, Bob and Betty told us that they didn't want to see Margaret climbing up into that big van. So, Bob handed me the keys to a beautiful 2000 Acura RL, with low mileage and all the bells and whistles that come on such a luxury car. Then the excitement exploded! We laughed, we prayed, we hugged, and we cried. Then we all jumped into that Acura for a late night tour of Greenville.

What a ride!

What a car!!

What friends!!!

THIRTY-SEVEN
Finding Your Gift

THEY SAY "There's one in every crowd." Well, I say you would have to have an enormous crowd in order to find one with the sense of humor, quick play on words, and sometimes subtle sarcasm accompanied by the cherubic smile of Ruth Ann Flower. Better known as Toodie, she is certainly one of a kind.

Dennis and Toodie Flower formed part of our missionary team for 42 years. We couldn't have asked for better coworkers and friends. Margaret and I treasure the years we had with them. Now 42 years is a long time—time enough to get well acquainted! Our team seldom lacked for humor. One visiting pastor from the U.S., in his parting farewell to our team, quipped, "When all other senses shall have departed, I am sure that in this team there shall still remain a sense of humor!" (His reference probably was not to Dennis.)

When our team moved to Burgos to plant a church, Dennis and I met at his apartment each afternoon for visitation and tract distribution. The first time I greeted Ruth Ann at the door with a happy "Howdy-doody, Toodie," she responded, without missing a beat, "What-do-you say, Flay?"

I recall one hot summer day when black ink from a *Time* magazine bled off on my hand. When I knocked on the Flowers' door, Toodie noticed the black smudge and said, "Well, Flay, now that you have *Time* on your hands, just have a seat. Dennis will be with you shortly."

I never could figure out what made her mind work the way it did. For the first few years as a team, I just figured that the purpose for her quick wit and "play on words" was to keep an element of amazement and humor in our work schedule. (Even though Spanish is Toodie's second language, she has the same quick wit and humor in Spanish that she has in English.)

Eventually, our team got involved in translating and publishing Majesty Music materials in Spanish. Toodie especially has a knack for translation. She does good work and is definitely a poet. When we started translating Ron Hamilton's Patch the Pirate materials, it dawned on me that God had a special purpose in giving her that unusual linguistic talent.

Are you familiar with the unusual character songs that Ron includes in his adventure stories? Here is an example of some of the "far out" ones:

Temper Tantrum Tilly
Poochie Lip Disease
Hippocritter
Wiggle Worm
Worry Warthog

Toodie has translated about 150 of Ron's adventure songs including the above. Folks, I have tried translating a few songs. It is work! Toodie puts in her hours. But even with that, it takes her rifle sharp wit to come up with a good singable translation that fits the style, rhythm, and spirit of Ron's imaginative songs.

When our Spain team, with the backing of Faith Christian Missions, Inc., published the Spanish hymnal, *Himnos Majestuosos*, Toodie translated 272 hymns. If we were to add up the Christmas and Easter cantatas as well as choral books, I would guess that she has translated over 700 hymns.

Ruth Ann Flower found her gift and is using it for God's honor and glory. Have you found your gift? If so, are you using it for His honor and glory?

THIRTY-EIGHT
Caught by Google

I MET beautiful Miss Margaret Amerson from Dothan, Alabama, during our freshman year at Bob Jones University. We were both work students and happily, from my point of view, were assigned to work the same set of tables in the dining room. Immediately, I was captivated by those sparkly blue eyes, her contagious smile, and her charming personality. From the very beginning I was convinced that Margaret could be a sure-win contestant for the title of "Miss Alabama." In fact, I bestowed the title of "Miss Alabama" upon her, and on the occasions when I could overcome my timidity, delighted in respectfully addressing her as such. Working with her in the dining common was a joy. I loved her artistic flare and her imaginative way of setting tables. I think I was "moonstruck" from the first day I met her.

Then, tragedy of tragedies, I soon learned that my Miss Alabama had begun dating my ugly roommate whom she had met a short time before I met her! To make matters worse, Margaret was unimpressed with me. I was an awkward hillbilly straight off of a North Carolina cotton farm. She delighted in calling me "ugly." "Hey, Ugly, would you put these glasses around the table for me," etc, etc. It looked to me like a hopeless case.

However, to make a long story short, Margaret and I were married in 1959. Five months later, my "Miss Alabama" and I had the privilege of going to Mexico for our first term of missionary service. Then we had the joy of serving four years in Chile.

"Miss Alabama's" fame was expanding.

From Chile, the Lord led us to Spain where I continued to brag on "Miss Alabama" who was always by my side.

After 42 years of ministry in Spain, we moved back to the USA. The Lord opened up a new ministry for us in a Hispanic church in Easley, SC, and I continue to talk to these Hispanics about my sweet "Miss Alabama." We are 82 years old now, and my beautiful bride is still by my side.

But, alas, technology has finally caught up with me. A curious lady named Griselda has spoiled everything. Without my permission, Griselda had the audacity to Google the "Miss Alabamas" all the way back to the time before Margaret and I started college. Margaret Amerson was not among the Miss Alabama queens! To protect my integrity, I had to go before the congregation and explain that, although Margaret does not officially hold the state title, to ME she is, was, and always will be, until death do us part, my "Miss Alabama" queen.

Thirty-Nine
Have You Considered Spain?

DURING THE 50+ years that Margaret and I have had the privilege of serving the Lord on the mission field, dozens of faithful missionaries have had an impact on our lives. Without doubt, the one who has most influenced us has been my coworker, Dennis Flower. I have known Dennis for over 50 years. We participated in evangelistic campaigns and music camps in Chile starting in 1964, and since we moved to Spain, Dennis and his wife, Ruth Ann, have been our constant companions in a close teamwork relationship. Someday I would like to write his inspiring story (unless I can convince him to do so).

In Dennis, as well as in many others, I have witnessed huge examples of faith, courage, and patience. There is no way that I can name all of these men and women much less write their stories. Nevertheless, I have chosen a family for this story and would like for it to be what I call a "generic tribute" to the many faithful and Godly servants who have been an example and inspiration to Margaret and me as our paths have crossed.

One week after arriving in Santiago, Chile, I was invited to direct the music for a Baptist youth camp. Lavon Waters, missionary to Uruguay, was the camp speaker. He proved to be a powerful preacher with a commanding voice and personality. God blessed in an unusual way that week. Hearts were touched, and lives were changed.

At the end of the week, Lavon asked me to pray about going to Uruguay two weeks later and directing the music in their youth camp. Since we had just arrived in Santiago and I had no other commitments, I decided to go. God also blessed in the Montevideo camp. There, I was privileged to meet Lavon's wife, Carolyn, and their three children: Connie, Joy, and David. Somehow, I sensed that those two weeks of working together in youth camps were just the beginning of a long friendship.

Sometime later I had the opportunity to take Margaret and our three daughters to Montevideo to meet the Waters family, and our friendship continued to grow. We were able to visit the most recent independent Baptist church that the Waters had planted in Montevideo. Margaret and our daughters met Wilson Caggiano and his wife Sarita. (I had met them at camp.) Lavon was training Brother Caggiano to be the next pastor and take over the ministry so the Waters would be free to move on to another area. The more we saw of their ministry, the more impressed we became. I gave Carolyn a few accordion lessons and encouraged her to continue to develop her musical abilities on the piano. Having already seen the importance of music on the mission field, I assured her that she would have many opportunities to teach others.

When we finished our four-year term in Chile, we again had a stopover in Montevideo with Lavon and Carolyn. Lavon had turned the church over to Pastor Caggiano and was getting ready to move and start another church. He told me that he was considering Paraguay or Bolivia. So I asked him, "Lavon, have you ever considered Spain?"

His answer was, "Frankly, no."

But by the next morning he had. He had prayed and had also written a letter to a missionary in Spain. Margaret and I were thrilled.

We flew on to the states for our furlough and then went to Spain for our third term. Within a few months, Lavon, Carolyn, and children arrived in Spain. Lavon's first goal was to plant an independent Baptist church in Madrid. They found a building in a suitable location and started visitation. God blessed their diligence. When Lavon had the inaugural service for the Calvary Baptist Temple (Templo Bautista Calvario) in Madrid, he invited me to lead the singing.

The church was going well, and soon Brother Lavon started sharing with some of us his burden for a fundamental

Baptist youth camp. The process of searching for property, red tape, frustrations, and discouragements would be a story by itself. Let me just say that as a result of a broad vision, deep burden, and faith that God would provide, the Waters started Mount Calvary Baptist Camp. The Lord led them to purchase an 18-acre tract of land in the province of Guadalajara, about an hour's drive outside the city of Madrid.

With the exception of the first summer when camp was only for Calvary Baptist Temple due to the lack of facilities, Emmanuel Baptist Church in Elche has taken young people, children, and adults to camp every summer. The camp has been a blessing and help to all of the independent Baptist churches in Spain. From our church, many young people have gone to camp and gotten saved. Others have been called into fulltime ministry. Two or three of our young people have found their husband or wife at camp!

Carolyn Waters wrote the words and I composed the music for the camp theme song. For many years, our church has included Mount Calvary Baptist Camp in our missions budget. When Margaret and I left Spain, we donated our accordion to camp to replace the one that had been stolen during a break-in.

After leaving his first church plant in Spain with a national pastor, Brother Lavon decided he needed to be closer to camp. A missionary had tried to start a church in Guadalajara, but after ten years only had one baptized member and three or four young people attending his meetings. After Brother Lavon agreed to take over that ministry, the other missionary moved to a different part of Spain to start over. Now that handful of people which Lavon inherited has grown to become a vibrant independent Baptist church with its own national pastor and a challenging missions program.

In his autobiography, *I Being in the Way, the Lord Led Me*, Dr. Frank Garlock lists in an appendix qualities he has observed in men who have been greatly used of God. One of his points is that "They have gone through the fire."

The list of personal losses and sicknesses that have plagued the Waters family in their more than 50 years on the mission field, reads like a bad novel:

- They lost a daughter in Uruguay, Patricia Karen, to spina bifida.
- Their doctor told them that the best therapy he knew of was to try to have another child. That pregnancy ended in a miscarriage.
- Their firstborn, Connie, met a dedicated young man in Bible College and they got married. They were making their plans to go to Spain as missionaries when Connie

became sick very suddenly. Two days later, she died with viral pneumonia.

- Their son, David, ended up in a hospital after having two convulsions in one day. He had to take anti-convulsion medicine for two years and was under a doctor's care.
- Their daughter, Joy, and her husband went to Spain as missionaries right out of college. Joy, at age 26 and mother of two, was diagnosed with Hodgkin's disease (cancer of the lymphatic system). Only after an extended period of chemotherapy and radiation treatments, the cancer was finally declared in remission.
- Lavon had a couple of serious hospital stays.
- When Carolyn was only 44, the doctor discovered that she had Polycystic Kidney Disease. God was gracious in giving her good health for many years, but the disease took its toll. Carolyn in her early seventies had to go on dialysis. However, in less than two years she had a kidney transplant and as of this writing, praise the Lord, she seems to be healthier than she was five years ago.

The Waters family has been through the fire. But the important thing is that, in spite of all their health issues and family losses, the Waters have stayed on the field and have not complained. Of course they have been discouraged, but not defeated.

In the midst of writing this tribute, I received a copy of their autobiography, *He Was Always by My Side*. Carolyn writes; "Did we ask why? You can be sure we did. . . . I have said many times that once I get to Heaven, I will ask Him why, but the more I think of it, the more I realize that then it won't even matter. . ."

Margaret and I have had a solid and edifying friendship with Lavon and Carolyn for almost 50 years. Recently, while they were on a whirlwind furlough to visit and report to supporting churches, they went out of their way to come to Greenville so we could have lunch together.

Lavon and I have not always agreed on methods. I am 100% for teamwork for missionaries, and I consider Lavon a loner. But God gave Lavon a vision for the lost and what needed to be done to win them. God gave him the patience and tenacity to stay with the job. I respect his work ethic. (Thank you, Lavon and Carolyn for your example to us.)

But my question is: Who will follow their example and come to take their place now that their strength is limited because of age?

As I already mentioned, there are many good missionaries who have faithfully served the Lord on the field for the long run. I could have written about Al and Helga Bonikowsky, who God has used to start two independent Baptist churches in the difficult Basque region of Northern

Spain. After 42 years of fruitful ministry in Spain, they retired in 2014. Who will take their place?

Marvin and Becky Robertson have had about four decades of fruitful ministry in the Madrid area, but they, too, have recently retired. Who will take their place?

That brings me back to my question to Lavon: HAVE YOU CONSIDERED SPAIN?

Spain still has a need for the Gospel and has a shortage of missionaries. Just as in Matthew 9, *the harvest truly is plenteous, but the laborers are few.* What are you willing to do about it?

A View From
Our Daughters

FORTY
Debbie

WHEN I think of growing up on the mission field, so many things come to mind. I think of humorous events as well as profoundly teachable moments that my parents used to make me and my sisters into the people we are today. Thanks to my dad's amazing spirit, I always viewed growing up on the mission field as an adventure and not a sacrifice.

By the time I was 18 years old, I had traveled in 28 countries and four continents! I got to visit some of the world's finest art museums, the Sistine chapel, Roman aqueducts, Gothic cathedrals, European palaces, Moorish architecture, as well as the beautiful natural mountains and landscapes of South America, Europe, and Africa.

Since we didn't have a PE class, Dad signed us up for swimming, judo, and horseback riding lessons. The opportunities we received more than compensated for things we missed from the U.S. My current job as a Spanish teacher is a direct result of learning Spanish as an MK.

I credit my dad's positive outlook on life and his constant reminder to see the challenges of life as an adventure instead of "suffering on the mission field" as the propelling factors in not feeling sorry for myself.

In fact, when I think of Dad, several humorous things come to mind.

Dad's jokes were so corny!! They were really bad, but we laughed anyway because he tried so hard to cheer us up. He must have gotten his humor from his brothers. They were always playing practical jokes on people. Dad's oldest brother, Bronner, built a go-kart. He engineered it so that, just for fun, they could change the winding on the steering wheel column so that when you turned it to the left, the go-kart would go to the right and when you turned the steering wheel to the right, it would go to the left. My dad and his brothers enjoyed letting their friends drive their go-kart, especially down a hill! They had so much fun!

When we were traveling to churches in the U.S., we spent a lot of time in the car. Inevitably we would get cranky or irritable after hours on the road. When the weather was bad, it was even worse; but Dad would have us sing a song that went like this: "With Christ in the Chevy we can smile at the storm, smile at the storm, smile at the storm. With Christ in the Chevy we can smile at the storm as we go riding on." It helped us create a positive focus.

When I graduated from high school, I was feeling a bit sorry for myself as I thought of other kids who had the opportunity to have a graduation ceremony, parties, send out graduation announcements, and receive gifts. My dad, seeing I was feeling a bit left out, decided to write up and print graduation announcements for me. He stated on the card that I WAS the class of 1979, and therefore I was class president, valedictorian, student body representative, and most likely to succeed. It was such a funny graduation announcement, I'm sure I received more gifts and money than most other seniors. I loved it!!

I don't really remember this, but Dad tells of an incident at bedtime when I was really young. We had a family practice that he would read us a bedtime Bible story, pray with us, and then tuck us in bed. One night I asked him if I could pray. He said "of course." I started my prayer just as I remembered Dad praying, but I got mixed up on a few details. I prayed "Dear Jesus, thank you for the food and help Daddy to be a good girl today. In Jesus' name, Amen."

On a slightly different note, I also remember walking into the living room and seeing my mom praying one day after her personal devotions. I tried to be very quiet so I wouldn't disturb her. I noticed that every few minutes she would pause, open her eyes, write something down on a piece of paper, and then keep praying. After she finished praying, I was curious as to what profound thoughts she might have been writing down while praying. I found the piece of paper and started reading. It was her grocery list!!

I also remember another incident that happened during prayer. After lunch we would have family devotion time where Dad would read the Bible to us, and then we would pray together as a family. My mom always had a long list of things to pray for. On Mondays she would pray for missionaries and mothers. On Tuesday she would pray for the team and teachers. On Wednesday she would pray for our supporting churches—and so on. Many times her prayers were very lengthy. One day while mom was praying, we heard a loud snore. Dad had fallen asleep during her prayer! My sisters and I thought it was hilarious, but my mom wasn't happy about it.

Mom and Dad had a way of making each of their daughters feel special. Every once in a while, Dad would proclaim me "Queen for the day." He would take me on a father-daughter date and buy me ice cream or some other special treat. He would do several wonderful things throughout the day to make me feel special. I loved those days.

My dad has a way of making other people feel special because he loves and cares for people. He is genuinely interested in others. At times this translated into people thinking he was "a slick talker" because he seemed to be able get his way with people. Actually when he showed a genuine interest in people and then made requests, they were much more willing to help him. On the mission field there were times when we needed to get government permits or licenses, and Dad had the ability to cut through "the red tape" just by how he treated others and got them to like him.

When I think of some of the things Dad tried to teach us, one thing that particularly comes to mind is loyalty.

My dad is a very loyal friend and husband. I remember being very upset and angry with my mom and complaining to my dad while he was driving me to my swimming class one afternoon. Instead of siding with me, the entire time he defended my mom and kept pointing out the wonderful qualities she had. I have seen him do that same thing when anyone tries to criticize his friends. He will overlook the bad and focus on the good.

The best thing about my dad is that I knew he loved me. No matter how I acted, I knew that would never change. He wouldn't hesitate to show his disappointment if I did something bad, but I never doubted his love. Along with his love for me, one of my dad's best attributes was that he was the same person inside the home behind closed doors as he was around a crowd of people. He never acted one way when people were around and another way when it was just family. He is genuinely the same person all the time. When you get to know my dad, you get to see the real him!

I hope this book has given you a "peek" into the exciting life we lived! I can proudly say it was a great joy to grow up on the mission field.

FORTY-ONE
Becky

IF I were to sum up my dad in three words, I would have to say "love," "humor," and "music." When I read I Corinthians 13, my dad is closer than anyone I know to fitting the descriptions of "patience, kindness, long-suffering, seeking not his own, believes all things, hopes all things, not easily provoked."

So many times I have seen a tear in his eye when he is simply talking of Jesus. Because of his love for his Lord, my mother, and others, he is so approachable. People were drawn to him and came to him for advice all the time. I remember him getting a call in the middle of the night from a family with a psychiatric daughter they could not control. He was able to go to the home, calm the daughter down, and help them avoid a crisis. I believe his being "raised on a farm with a large family" had a big influence on the unassuming way in which he interacts with others. I'm sure he got a lot of his humor from the farm life as well.

As a child, I remember so many times when he turned "hardships" into adventures. Rather than think we had things bad, he made us feel like we were "pioneers." If we got hurt, we were "tough" and could handle it. During a camping trip in Portugal, when a bad storm blew our tent away, we had the "adventure" of seeking shelter at the campground bath house. Dad always made the impossibly bad situations simply seem like "exciting challenges." He could turn an insult into a compliment, and anger into laughter.

My dad's passion for music also started when he was a young boy, growing up in a musical family. That passion has never left him, and he has used his musical talent as an inroad for the Gospel, bringing people into church who were drawn by their interest in music and then introduced to the Lord. From writing love songs to my mother, or "wake up; it's time to go to school" songs for us girls to songs of praise to the Lord, music has played a huge part in his life.

I see my dad as an uncomplicated man—single-minded in his love for God, family, and others; finding humor even in difficult circumstances; and making life more colorful and beautiful through music. Having those three qualities, he has made a huge impact on my life and I'm sure on many others as well.

FORTY-TWO
Mimi

MY EARLIEST memories of the mission field were when we were living in Chile. I remember church services, singing Spanish hymns and choruses, children's clubs in our back yard, and the day that Mom led me to the Lord. She explained to me that just being born into a Christian family didn't automatically make me a Christian, and I realized that I needed to personally ask the Lord to save me. I'm grateful to my parents for the attitude they transmitted to us—that it was a great privilege to serve the Lord as missionaries.

When religious liberty laws were passed in Spain permitting missionaries to go there legally, Dad was led to go through that new open door of service. I remember as an 8-year-old being very excited that our family had the privilege of being one of the first missionaries to go to Spain. We never felt like we were missing out.

Furloughs were great times to travel and meet people. We stayed in many homes. In most of them, Dad would tune the piano, and we'd all sit around singing songs and telling stories. Of course Dad always managed to sing a few of the love songs he had written to Mom.

On the field, Dad and Mom sacrificed to provide music and sports opportunities for us. I remember monthly four-hour trips to Madrid for flute lessons with Mrs. Carol West, which also included Dad giving her son, Jim, trombone lessons. (Jim continued in music and, since college, has played trombone in several brass bands and symphony orchestras.) Dad created a school band for us missionary kids (11 MKs on the team). We even prepared a concert that we performed at the town square in Quintanadueñas.

Debbie, Becky and I took piano lessons from "Uncle Dennis" Flower. He required five hours a week of practice in order to have a lesson, and I don't remember ever going a week without one, thanks to Mom's insistence! Since he didn't charge for the lessons, Mom also had us girls take turns preparing a dessert for our teacher. Dad was always preparing music for us to do in church, and Mom had us get involved in the children's Bible clubs.

When doctors told my parents that we twins had scoliosis and needed to swim regularly, we joined a military sports club. At the time we didn't enjoy swimming in the rather cold indoor pool, but we were thrilled to be able to take horseback riding lessons with Don Pepe. We had bikes, skates, and when we were older, a 49cc motor bike that we would ride out in the country. Dad installed a chin-up bar for us, and at church we had a ping-pong table that provided tons of fun.

Yearly camping trips gave us the opportunity to travel to several countries in Europe. We packed our food, air mattresses, sleeping bags and tent, and stayed at campgrounds. Over the years we met people at these campgrounds that came and visited us at our home. We gave them the Gospel, and some were saved.

As teenagers, our home was "grand central station" for the young people from church.

One of my fondest memories, though, is the talks we had around our kitchen table. We talked about right and wrong philosophies and world views, and of course Dad told us stories. I've always loved his stories, and I'm excited that now I'll have them for my children and grandchildren! Many of the qualities I most love about my dad show up in the stories told in this book.

Several things come to mind as I think about Dad's influence on my life. One special trait was his love. As a young girl, I would go to him with all my worst struggles—those awful, embarrassing ones as well as the plain, foolish ones. I could count on his unconditional love and attention.

Another important example he set for me was his cheerful problem-solving attitude towards life. Complications or obstacles that sprung up before us as a family immediately became a challenge to be met head on with joy and optimism.

Finally, I have always valued his advice on how to be a friend to others. His direction in this area has been a huge help to me in our mission field in the Basque region of Spain.

Ultimately, Dad's desire has been to glorify God with his life, and that has helped us girls follow him in loving and trusting our Heavenly Father.

Appendix

To receive further information about ordering *Himnos Majestuosos*, contact:

Faith Christian Missions, Inc.
P. O. Box 1883
Dothan, AL 36302
faithchristianmissions@juno.com
1-334-793-4579
www.faithchristianmissions.org

Or

Majesty Music
733 Wade Hampton Blvd.
Greenville, SC 29609
1-800-334-1071
1-864-242-6722
www.majestymusic.com

Additional materials

- Missionary cantata (with book and CD):
  Here Am I, Lord
    Samuel Flay Allen
    Majesty Music - www.majestymusic.com

- *Hymn Arrangements for the Classical Guitar*
    Samuel Flay Allen
    Majesty Music

- *Just a Minute*
    Andy Bonikowsky
    www.countingthestars.org

- *The Aierdi Miracle* (English or Spanish)
    Andy Bonikowsky
    www.countingthestars.org

CPSIA information can be obtained at www.ICGtesting.com
Printed in the USA
LVOW11s2239201016

509642LV00001B/3/P